altho I ha[...]
befo[r]e, my [...]
of living out beginning with
Kit Hammett. This is
a juvenile book or rather

"Perhaps you have read tales of the people who lived in the early days of America—the Indians, explorers, woodsmen. They were America's first campers; they have left people of today a heritage that makes them want to get out of doors, to know and enjoy the creatures and things that live there. They have left a challenge, too, to make good use of our camping lands and forests. Those of us who live in cities and towns have much to learn before we can enjoy to the full the woods and the out-of-doors. That learning is the beginning of the campcraft trail.

"This book is planned to help you develop those campcraft skills that will make you a good camper. Each skill can lead to fascinating new trails and activities, either separately, or all woven together into one great adventure of camping."

—See Chapter 1.

for the young, but
not be be belittled.
Kit was a fair person.

LHS

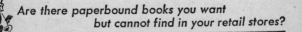

YOUR OWN BOOK OF
Campcraft

Prepared under the auspices of
the American Camping Association

by CATHERINE T. HAMMETT

Illustrated by
LOUIS AND SAM GLANZMAN

PUBLISHED BY POCKET BOOKS NEW YORK

YOUR OWN BOOK OF CAMPCRAFT

POCKET BOOK edition published July, 1950
29th printing.........March, 1972

This original POCKET BOOK edition is printed from
brand-new plates made from newly set, clear, easy-to-read type.
POCKET BOOK editions are published by POCKET BOOKS, a division of
Simon & Schuster, Inc., 630 Fifth Avenue, New York, N.Y. 10020.
Trademarks registered in the United States and other countries.

L

CONTENTS

CHAPTER 1

"Come on Out!"

COME ON OUT! Out for a picnic, out for a hike, out to go camping in the woods, out to cook a hamburger or out just to be lazy under the sun and blue sky! COME ON—let's go out somewhere!

Did you ever bake a potato in the coals of an outdoor fire, eating it so hot you could hardly hold it? Did you ever spend the night in a pup tent, waking up sometime in the early morning to wonder at the brightness of the stars? Did you ever put a pack on your back, hike up hill and down and reach the end of the trail feeling tired but oh! so *good*? Did you ever sit around a campfire, singing or swapping yarns, while the fire crackled? If you have, it is a sure thing that you felt it was "tops"; if you have never done any such thing, it is just as sure that you've sometimes wished you could. Most of us are campers at heart and like nothing better than getting out of doors for the adventure that is there.

Hiking and camping give you many chances for the best of outdoor activities and fun. Whether you camp by a lake, go by canoe along quiet inland waterways, climb a mountain, ride a horse over prairie country, drive a trailer to new camping land, or join some organized summer camping group, you know that living outdoors can be the best possible way of spending vacation time. But, outdoor fun can begin at home, in your club or troop, too, and day trips to nearby spots can give you a taste of the adventure that is in store when you can go farther afield.

Perhaps you have read tales of the people who lived in the early days of America—the Indians, the explorers, the woodsmen, the families of the covered wagon treks. They were America's first campers; they have left young people of today a heritage that makes them want to get out of doors, to know and enjoy the creatures and things that live there. They have left a challenge, too, to make good use of our natural resources, camping lands and forests. Those of us who live in cities and towns have much to learn before we can enjoy to the full the woods and the out-of-doors, which were thoroughly familiar to this country's earliest settlers. We must begin to develop skills that will help us learn how to live outdoors. Some of us can go to summer camps, others can go camping with their families, and still others can find town hiking and exploring groups. But all must start with learning skills—and that learning is the beginning of the camp-craft trail.

Every kind of game and sport has its experts and its beginners; in between there are lots of people who are just average or a little better. None of them can say they are good at the game unless they know the rules and can play it skillfully. You don't wear a football helmet when you play tennis; you don't play baseball with hockey sticks; you don't "serve" in basketball; you don't "kick off" in archery; you don't "make a run" in bowling. Every sport or hobby has its particular rules of playing, its particular equipment, and its high standards of GOOD performance. Camping has, too, and while many people may go outdoors and have a good time there, they are not considered GOOD campers if they lack the knowledge of what to do and how to do it. In camping there are rules of the woods for good performance, equipment that brands you as an expert, tricks and skills that show that you are "big league." GOOD campers are concerned with conservation of natural resources; they know how to build fires easily, how to control them, how to cook a meal that is done to a turn. CAMPCRAFT is the art or skill of being a good camper; for most, campcraft means the very first things learned that lead to more advanced outdoor fun.

This book is planned to help you develop those campcraft skills that will make you a good camper. They are just the very first steps, but each one can lead to fascinating new trails and activities, either separately, or all woven together into one great adventure of camping.

One thing about camping is that you seldom can do it without bearing a real responsibility for other people or property. You cannot go on a hike, build a fire, pitch a tent, or follow a trail without using private or public forests or parks of which we are the custodians. The way we use these lands for camping has a relation to other people. A good camper knows not only how to make an outdoor fire, but how to control it; he knows not only how to chop down a tree, but how to choose the tree so that the forest is not harmed.

Just as in tennis, or baseball, or photography, or any other hobbies—the more you know, the more fun you have; in camping you have many, many trails of adventure to follow as you learn more of campcrafting and of forest lore. Here are campcrafting ways to help you as you start down the trails——

WHERE TO HAVE OUTDOOR FUN

An Indian boy hunted and fished as part of his daily living; learning to shoot a bow and arrow was part of his schooling. Boys and girls of log cabin days helped to build their homes and, as part of their everyday chores, to get wood for the fire. Today we must go away from home to hike, to camp, or to learn about nature. Many people erroneously think they must go far away, and so seldom have the fun they might have. There are good outdoor places even in a city, and many chances even to learn outdoor skills indoors. Anyone can begin to learn about camping, no matter where he may be—and when he finds himself in real camping country, he will have a far better time because of all he knows.

IN THE CITY—Get outdoors in the parks, on rooftops, in yards. If you live in a small town or on the edge of a city, you may have a spot

where you and your club or troop can build a
fireplace. If you have a club or troop, your
meeting place may offer chances for some outdoor fun. Walks around the streets in suburban
towns, visits to estates that have interesting trees
and bushes, and day trips out of town to nearby
parks and forests are always possible. In New
York City there are camping sites on the roofs
of skyscrapers; in Chicago you can get to a forest
preserve from downtown in less than an hour's
bus trip; in many smaller places you can get to
open spaces by a fairly short walk. Don't let city
streets and tall buildings keep you indoors! There
are plenty of places to enjoy outdoor fun—anywhere!

IN CAMP—Some of you will have the chance
to go camping—with your family, with your
troop or with your club. You will find all sorts
of chances for outdoor adventures there. The
campcrafting skills that are mentioned here may
help you to prepare yourself for a mountain trip
of several days, a trip on horseback or by canoe.
When you do go to camp—whether for overnight or for many weeks,—take the chance that
is there to do *real* outdoor things, the things
that are hard to do alone or in the city.

CHAPTER 2

On the Trail

"I'M HAPPY WHEN I'M HIKING, PACK UPON MY BACK—," so goes a song that campers often sing as they swing along the trail. Hiking is one of the best of outdoor activities, perhaps because it combines so many parts of outdoor fun—adventure, good exercise, outdoor cooking, trailing, exploring, and many others. There are all sorts of hikes; they range from the short afternoon's walk to a mountain climbing trip, and in between lie many different trails.

PLANNING

Individuals, families, camp groups or in-town groups get *extra* fun from making plans and preparations and learning outdoor skills indoors on the days between hikes. Most of us cannot get out into the country as often as we would like to, so it helps stretch outdoor fun to do things beforehand. You can learn about interesting things to be seen along the trail, you can develop skills to help you enjoy the woods. You can pack and repack, to be sure you have just the right things to take;—and you will find that well-laid plans will pay off in a better kind of a day, once you are off.

Your very first hike may be the beginning of a hobby that will last a lifetime! So go at it right, to begin with! There are many hiking, mountain and trail clubs whose members have found new and interesting things to do out of doors. Some of these groups have junior organizations. There are national and local organizations, such as the Appalachian Mountain Club and the Sierra Mountain Club, with local chapters. In fact, in almost any town there are clubs whose activities include opportunities for getting out in the open. Sometimes nature groups, such as the Audubon Society, combine nature with hiking and field trips with camping.

HIKING has been described as "walking with a will"; for campcrafters it generally means getting about under your own steam, by foot, by bike, by horseback, in a canoe—generally in groups. As you grow in skill, you may advance to mountain or rock climbing. But for most of you, hiking will mean day trips, or perhaps an overnight camp, so these next pages will help with such first steps.

Why not get some hiking enthusiast to tell you some of his adventures? Or perhaps you can talk with someone who has gone hosteling, or on a canoe trip, or over a long horseback trail. Perhaps someone can show you slides or movies to help you catch the wonderful feeling of being away from everything, high on a hill, or deep in the wilderness. Your first hikes will be setting the stage for just such adventures for you.

There are many places where hikers and campers can go, where there are shelters and places to cook. The American Youth Hostel Association* maintains just such places at a very small cost; your group can get a group membership, or you may join as an individual. State and Federal parks and forests often have camping spots or hiking places. Find out what there is that you can use, in your own town, or nearby—and begin to plan making use of it all. There is no need to stay home!

Whether your family is going on a picnic, your troop on a Saturday hike, or your club off for a weekend trip to a summer cottage, someone will need to make plans. You'll be off to a bad start if you get to the meeting place and discover that half the gang didn't know when to meet. It is worse to start preparing lunch only

* Address—National Headquarters, 6 East 39th St., New York 19, N. Y.

to discover that no one brought the meat. And it is hard on your mother if she doesn't know when to expect you home. All this means— MAKE A PLAN. Every one who is going may have a hand in planning, or you may have several committees to do the planning; it's more fun for every one to have a part in *some* of it. Here are some suggestions on what to think about:

For any hike or short trip, talk over and decide:

> where to go—when and how
> what to take
> how it will be packed and carried
> what to wear
> what to do on the way, and when you arrive
> how to divide jobs
> how to walk on the highway—your outdoor
>   manners
> how to clean up—at the hike site and back
>   home

If you are planning an overnight hike or camp, add these to the list given above:

> Plan for well-balanced meals, including how
>   to pack, carry and store food. (See chapter
>   on *Outdoor Food*.)
> Plan for the making of camp, including shelter, equipment, how to make camp, how to
>   strike it at end.

If you go to some place that has some equipment, be sure to find out WHAT, before you complete your plans.

Plan sleeping arrangements, including how to pack and carry. (See pages 24-27 for making a bed roll.)

Plan personal equipment, including how to pack and carry.

Work up to an overnight trip. If your group has not done much hiking, plan several short or easy jaunts to help you get ready for a longer one. All your campcrafting skills will be put to a test on an overnight hike—so be sure you have the skills before you go! Perhaps these steps will help you get ready.

Cook several different meals in your outdoor kitchen.

Go on at least one all-day hike—dressed properly, carrying your own food and equipment.

Sleep outdoors on a straw tick, a cot, or a sleeping bag. Sleep on the ground at least once, near camp or home.

Go on a two-meal trip or hike, carrying everything you need, taking care of the second meal's food, etc.

Learn to make a blanket roll or a pack.

You should be ready by now!

Here are some suggestions to help in making plans:

WHERE TO GO

—to city parks, reservations, forests, sanctuaries, etc.

—to *private property* where you can get permission to use the land. Groups may often have the use of a corner of someone's property as a permanent place for hikes and camps.

—to *camps* belonging to local organizations. (Ask around to see if there are any you may use.)

—by bus, car, or train to *state or federal parks* or forests where there may be trails for hiking, camping spots, or overnight shelters.

—just out in the *open country,* along dirt roads, off main highways. Local newspapers often outline such trips in the spring and fall; watch for such interesting items.

—to *points of historical or local interest;* get to know your own countryside.

To find out what is available, get in touch with local organizations and such agencies as park and recreation departments, state forest or park officials, and federal agencies, such as the U. S. Forest Service. Some organizations have suggestions for short day trips, giving routes, costs, etc.

As far as possible—go under your own steam!

Make it a HIKE!

WHAT TO EAT

See the chapter on *Outdoor Food* for this—whether you plan to carry your lunch ready-made, or to cook it on the trail.

WHAT TO TAKE

This depends on what you plan to do. For a day's trip, take a lunch, or the food for it (concentrated food is lighter to carry). For other equipment—a knife, a first aid kit, a cup, a notebook, a sketchbook or your camera, a map and compass may be the things you will need.

If you are cooking, take matches and what utensils you will need; tools, too, such as a hand axe, if you will need it.

Pack your lunch and equipment in a knapsack. Carry it over your shoulder, on your back, or on your belt. Let your hands be free to help you swing along the trail.

You may need permission for using fireplaces or for building fires in certain areas at certain times of the year. Check with your local park and fire departments to be sure about this. When picnic places are crowded, it is sometimes well to have such a permit to be sure you will have a place to cook.

You may not "take" a permit to use other people's property, but it is good outdoor manners to ask permission before crossing or using such property.

Plan for safe water. Carry a little bottle of Clorox with a medicine dropper. Two drops of Clorox in a gallon of water will make it safe to drink.

WHAT TO WEAR

This, too, depends on what you are going to do, as well as on the climate, season, and the probable weather for the day. Mainly, it is important just to use your head! Avoid too much or too little; too much will be a burden, too little will have painful results, and either will spoil your fun. Get advice from the experts in your locality.

Don't go fancy! Old, comfortable clothes that help you enjoy the outdoors with freedom of action and freedom from care are the best. Wear things that won't get snagged, that are strong but light, and that tend to be roomy rather than tight.

In general—plan for the kind of activity and the kind of weather you are apt to meet.

In the *fall*, the days will be warm, but as soon as the sun goes down, you'll need a sweater or jacket.

In the *winter*, several layers of light-weight wool will keep you warmer than one very heavy layer, and you can take layers off or put them back on as you need them.

For *sun*, keep head, shoulders, and legs cov-

ered when moving in the sun (go at sun-tanning
gradually)! Peel off shirts when resting in the
shade. Wear sun visors or glasses when on the
road.

For *cross country*, or rough going, wear jeans
or smooth-material slacks that won't catch burrs;
protect arms and legs from briars and branches.

For *snow*, wear light-weight, warm ski and
snow suits. Plan extra socks for the time when
you come indoors again; wear waterproof shoes
and mittens.

For *wind*, wear closely woven jackets and
slacks, a scarf at your neck, and knitted or tight
cuffs at wrists and ankles.

For *rain*, in the summer it probably doesn't
matter—if you can change to dry clothes when
you stop walking. For cooler days, put a light-
weight rain jacket or coat in your pack. Water-
repellent jackets serve many purposes, and are
especially useful in unexpected showers. Plan
something to cover your head, and to keep rain
from going uncomfortably down your neck!

For *hiking*, wear shoes that are comfortable
(NOT NEW) and that give good support; they
should be roomy, but not too large; wear one or
two pairs of wool socks—with no darns and holes.
(Take extra socks, no matter what else you take.)
For heavy hiking, be sure soles of shoes are heavy.
NEVER start out with shoes with soles that are
beginning to rip, or are thin; you'll be sorry.

For *bicycling* and cross country, girls will want to tie their hair back or to wear a kerchief to keep their hair from blowing. Clip jeans or slacks at ankles. Keep knees covered on first jaunts in sun!

For *mountain-climbing* and more advanced activities, get advice before you begin to build your camping wardrobe.

For *overnight camping* trips—go as light as you can; use dark shirts and jeans; take extra socks and underwear—plan to stop long enough to wash in a brook, if necessary.

WHAT TO DO ON THE WAY or WHEN YOU ARRIVE

This depends, too, on where you go, and what is around, but in general make the most of being out of doors, and do the things you can't do in town or in other seasons.

See what there is to see—of historical or local interest; of natural interest. Look up exhibits, trail museums, markers, etc.

Plan time on the way to see around you—the scenery, the people, the birds and trees and insects. A *hike* offers great chances for this—don't speed along as if you were off for a big trip.

If you are planning a particular destination, chart your time along the way, so you can do these things on the way. Go and return by different routes, if you can. Plan about getting back; it is part of the hike.

If you plan to stay at one spot most of the day, you will want to get there in the most direct fashion and will plan the time while there to learn new skills, try out old or new tricks, cook something that takes some time, sit around and talk, play games, etc. Be ready to change everything if some fine new adventure turns up; you may have a chance to watch some ants moving their home, or playing horseshoes may be such fun you don't want to stop—being outdoors means leisurely hours, just to have fun!

DIVIDING JOBS

If every one tries to make the fire, help cook, and lead in games, you'll all end up by being mad! Besides, not everybody needs to be working all the time, so some can play horseshoes, sit by the brook, climb trees or skip stones while others are doing jobs that need doing. Unless you know what is your share, though, you don't always feel free to wander off, or sit and read. Dividing up jobs is the answer.

Some people make charts that give every one a job; others count off, assigning jobs to numbers; others like to let people choose, being sure that making the fire does not always go to the expert, but rather to those who need to learn how. Cleaning up is always the worst job, and some provision needs to be made for that; it really should be everyone's job, and if everyone is careful not to throw things around, there isn't much to be done.

When there is a crowd, you may divide something like this:

FIRE MAKERS—Arrange fireplace, woodpile, etc. Make and keep fire. (Generally everyone else gets wood, first thing.)

COOKS—Prepare and serve meals, or arrange food, out of the way of insects, animals and humans. Each person can get his own when it is time to eat. For big crowds this is quite a job. You may divide again, having another group that arranges the table for food and utensils.

PROGRAM—There may be need of a group to plan the activities of the day, to lead in these activities, to plan the campfire, etc.

CLEAN-UPS—Even when everyone pitches in, there needs to be a special squad to supervise, to plan how it will be done. They see that the site is left better than they found it; they check to be sure the fire is out, the rubbish completely burned, etc.

When planning for any kind of hike or camp, plans should be made beforehand about what will happen when you first reach the site. Generally the place is "settled" for the day; food put away in a cool, dry, ant-free place; fireplaces and kitchens put in readiness; jackets and other equipment stored in a dry place.

For overnight camps, this is even more necessary; get the most important group necessities taken care of—the cooking place, food storage place, shelters for night, latrine and washing place. Divide the jobs into those that one or two do for the group, and those that each camper does for himself.

If you make plans for a hike, with your club or group, the plans may look something like this:

WHERE WE'LL GO—Destination

How long will it take to get there?

How do we go? (Hike all the way? Bus part way? etc.)

Time to leave

Time to return

Cost, if any

WHAT WE'LL DO— On the way

At the site

On the way home

WHAT SHOULD WE LEARN BEFOREHAND?

WHAT TO TAKE?   FOOD   EQUIPMENT

WHO WILL BRING?   MENU PLANNED

Program supplies or equipment

WHO WILL DO WHAT?
  Wood gatherers
  Fire builders and cooks
  Clean-ups
  etc.
	CHECK LIST FOR
	  EACH PERSON
	    carfare?
	    food?
	    equipment?
	    knife?
	    compass?
	    sweater?
	    etc.
	    etc.

CHAPTER 3

Your Own Outdoor Equipment

YOU begin to collect your own camping and hiking equipment when you get your first jackknife! You'll progress until you have something like a fine down-filled sleeping bag that weighs almost nothing, but is warm as can be. Much of your equipment you can assemble or make yourself; there are many kinds that you will buy. It's the campcrafting way to make your own—even small tents and sleeping bags. Such pieces of equipment are more advanced than this book, but you will want to progress to them. The Boy Scout and Explorer Scout books can help you on this; get a scout to help you.

WHAT YOU NEED

A *bandana handkerchief* is a campcrafter's best friend—for a pot holder, a brow-wiper, a towel, something to wrap your lunch in, or something for treasures you are bringing home. You'll want a bright one to hang on your belt—or on a stick, hobo fashion.

A *hike kit* will come next—a knapsack for your back or a bag to go on one shoulder or to hang on your belt. Make one out of good heavy material like denim or lightweight canvas. Make it fit your plate and cup and little frying pan. Put pockets in it for your lunch or your knife and fork. Make it *sturdy*—for hard use. Stitch on a sewing machine, or use strong cord and a large needle.

Have your hike kit ready for any occasion—it will be easier to get going if it is all ready, hanging on a peg, just waiting for an outdoor day.

Your *belt*, with clips for knife, compass and whistle, may be next on your list. You'll soon be wanting an axe, too.

Little *bags* for food or for personal equipment are good to make, too.

Leather *sheaths* for knives and axes are good craft projects.

A *first aid kit* is a necessity for any outing. Knowledge of what to do is necessary, too. Plan your kit to take care of things that may happen, and get a doctor or nurse to tell you how to treat cuts and scratches, bruises, burns, sprains, etc. You can make your own first aid kit or buy one ready-made.

If you plan overnight hikes and camping, you will need a *waterproof ground sheet*. You may buy or borrow a "poncho," a rubberized or waterproofed cloth that can be used as a tent or a ground sheet. You can waterproof your own with waterproofing liquid (purchased at hardware stores) or by rubbing with paraffin, then pressing with a hot iron.

You will want *pup tents* or hike tents, for one or two campers. Pup tents can be purchased at little cost at army surplus stores; it is an advanced project to make your own. See the Boy Scouts' camping book for good help on this.

A *sleeping bag* or blanket roll will complete your sleeping arrangements.

As you and your club grow more experienced, you may make pack baskets, knapsacks, pack boards, paddles, bicycle packs, or many other things you will need.

There's no feeling like that proud feeling of a good, well-made piece of equipment—something that you have made yourself!

Learn to take good care of your equipment, store it away after each trip; it will repay you many times.

Talk with some one who goes camping every year; he will tell you how much planning he puts into his equipment. He will tell you what he thinks is important, and he can help you know what to begin to collect as your camping and hiking gear.

When you and your family begin to get camping gear for a family trip, you'll want easily transported items. Perhaps you and your dad will make a trailer for your gear.

Your gang or patrol may make a start at equipment, jointly made and owned. Light-weight tents, boxes that carry food and then become cupboards, nested kettles—all will be considered in your planning.

For canoe trips, horseback trips, mountain climbing trips, you'll want specialized equipment that you can pack and carry with ease. Talk to experts on this!

MAKING AN ENVELOPE BED ROLL

For an overnight hike or for any camping trip, prepare your bed at home before starting out. An envelope or Klondike bed keeps you warm because you have blankets under and over you— and you cannot kick them off! Use this method for any cold night, indoors or out.

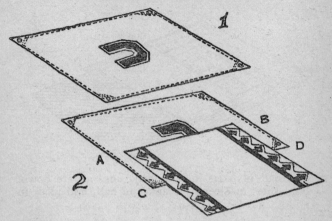

1. Place poncho flat on ground.

2. Place first blanket with one edge down center of poncho. (A-B)

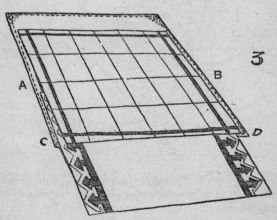

3. Place second blanket with one edge at *middle* of first blanket. (C-D)

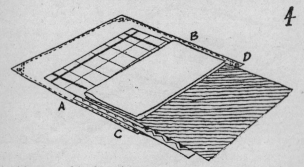

4. Alternate blankets in same way, until all are down. Fold sheet or sleeping blanket in half, and place in middle. (A-B-C-D)

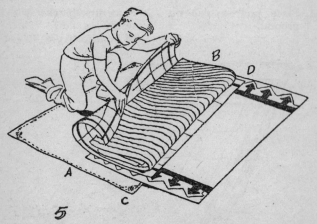

5. Starting with last blanket you put down, fold blankets, alternating in reverse order, until all are over middle. (A-B-C-D)

Pin with blanket pins at bottom, if poncho does not snap together, or fold under.

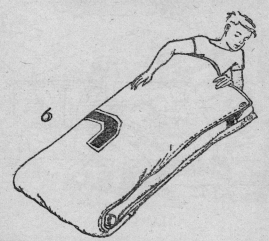

6. Fold poncho over. Snap together, if there are snaps on bottom and side.

Wriggle down from the top, getting in the middle of the sleeping blanket or sheet.

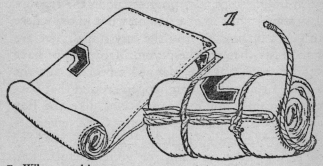

7. When packing up, put your night things and toilet articles inside and roll from bottom.

See page 99 for knots to tie.

CHAPTER 4

Campcraft Skills

NO matter how much you like outdoor fun, you can't learn everything at once, so start with simple steps, and progress along the trail by easy stages. Just in case you may not know where to begin or how to find the easy stages, here are some tests that will help you. Many camps have similar tests that are planned especially for the kinds of things that can happen around that particular camp; some organizations, like the Boy and Girl Scouts and the Campfire Girls, have outdoor tests for badges or honors. If you do not have such help in your camp or your organization, you will find it lots of fun to start being a *camp-crafter*, and then a *pioneer*, a *woodcrafter* and a *frontiersman.* If your family is planning to go camping next summer, you all may like to work on some progressive steps together. If your club or school grade is planning a camping experience, or if you and your gang want to see how well you can measure up against each other, you will find these helpful.

You will see that there are four steps—each with various activities that will help you be a good all-around camper. Remember that just passing a test never means much, unless you can use what you have learned—unless it leads you on to more interesting activities. Whether you check by yourself or work with other boys and girls, you will be on the right trail if you go along these lines. (There is a chapter in this book to help with each step.)

Check lists like this can never be made to meet all the varying conditions and situations in all parts of the country and in all camps and groups. If you find that something is much more important in your section, or more interesting because of what grows there, or the kind of country it is, substitute that in place of what is here. If you are a member of a club or camp or group, you may want to make up a whole new set of activities. And don't stop with the fourth list! There are many, many more skills and activities to beckon you on down the campcraft trail.

Have fun!

Check List	CAMPCRAFTER
	Help prepare a good safe place for an outdoor fire. Gather tinder, kindling and fuel, and light a foundation fire, keeping it burning for at least three minutes.
	Cook, so it looks and tastes good, one thing like toast and one thing like cocoa or a one-pot dish.
	Show that you know how to care for and use a knife, and make something like shavings, a toasting stick or a pin with a knife you have sharpened.
	Show that you know how to make and use two knots.
	Have your own hiking kit for outdoor meals, and know how to take good care of it.

Help make plans for a picnic, hike, or cookout, including what to take, where to go, what to do, etc.	
Show that you know how to dress properly to go outdoors in your locality. Show that you know how to hike on the open road. Go on a two-mile hike.	
Show that you know three rules of good outdoor citizenship for your part of the country.	
Get acquainted with something in nature—a tree, a bird, an animal, etc. Observe it.	
Watch a sunrise, a sunset, or a storm gathering.	
Know how to find NORTH by stars and by the sun.	
Find a story, a poem, a picture, etc. that describes something you like in the out-of-doors.	

Check List	PIONEER
	Tell six points of fire safety for your locality. Show that you can build two types of fires, such as criss cross and tepee, and know when they are used.
	Cook successfully by two different types of cooking—broiling, baking, etc. Plan a well-balanced meal using them.
	Show that you know how to get fuel for a woodpile, using a bucksaw and sawbuck, or similar tools used in your locality. Help make a woodpile.
	Show that you know how to make and use two types of lashing.
	Add something to your own camping equipment, such as a poncho, sleeping bag, knapsack, and know how to use and care for it. Make some piece of equipment.

Help make plans for a day's trip, with one meal cooked out, planning how to pack, carry and take care of food.	
Go on the hike, properly equipped, carrying own equipment, food, etc.	
Show that you know three points of conservation of natural resources for your locality. Do something to help conservation.	
Choose something in nature to learn more about—trees, stars, birds, etc. Learn several general facts about them, and several specific facts about some you have observed.	
Know how to set and sight with a compass.	
Know a good hiking song and a song about the out-of-doors.	

Check List	WOODCRAFTER
	Help with a fire for a beanhole, a barbecue or some special cookout.
	Lay a fire in an indoor fireplace and light it successfully.
	Cook successfully by two new types of cooking you have not shown before, such as reflector baking, aluminum foil, Dutch oven baking, etc.
	Show that you know how to care for and to use a small axe (hand axe or two-handed axe). Split a small log into kindling.
	Know the knots to use in tying a blanket roll, or a pack.
	Show that you know how to pack a pack or a pack basket, make a blanket roll or envelope bed, or whatever is used in your locality. Tell about your favorite piece of camping equipment.

Help make plans for a two-meal trip, including well-balanced meals, equipment, etc.	
Go on the hike. Begin to learn how to get around the country, in whatever way is generally used in your locality (hiking, canoeing, etc.).	
Show that you know five things a camper can do to protect living things. Help something grow.	
Learn something new about nature from reading in a book, talking with a nature enthusiast, or observation. Share your knowledge with your group.	
Know how to follow a map and how to make a simple sketch map.	
Read a story or article about some outdoor project, hobby, activity or interesting happening, or take or sketch an outdoor picture.	

Check List	FRONTIERSMAN
	Lay a ceremonial campfire—and light it successfully (later) or know something more about the type of fires used in your locality.
	Help plan and cook an outdoor meal without adult supervision during the preparation.
	Show some kind of progress in using tools used in your locality. Show you know good conservation in selecting your project.
	Make a belt or a net, a splicing, or some article using knots and lashings.

Help pitch a wall tent, or help make an overnight camping site.	
Help plan and carry out a two- or three-day trip, using nearby facilities. (Perhaps it will be on horseback, by bicycle, on foot, in canoes.)	
Know the "conservation pledge" and learn something of the work of your state or federal conservation and forestry services.	
Keep a nature diary for several weeks, making daily entries of things you see and hear that interest you.	
Go cross-country with map and compass for at least a mile.	
Tell a story, teach a song, plan a ceremony or campfire activity about the out-of-doors.	

CHAPTER 5

Fire Building and Fireplaces

FIRE—your good friend and servant in the out-of-doors. There is nothing a campcrafter enjoys more, or uses more than a fire, from that glowing campfire to sit around in the dark to the quick hot fire that boils water. Fire is a good servant when under control. So, while appreciating all a fire does, it is important to realize what YOU must do to control it. Care of the fire and fire prevention become *responsibilities* of any one who lights a match in the open—and so a good campcrafter knows not only how to light a fire, but also how to put it out.

Fire has many uses: to cook food, heat water, destroy rubbish, and give warmth. A campcrafter learns to make a beginning or foundation fire, and how to build that into different types of fires for various uses.

A GOOD fire
1) is built in a safe place which helps control it;
2) is just large enough to serve the need
   and to make thrifty use of wood;
3) is kept under control, and is watched
   at all times;
4) is put OUT when no longer needed.

Most fires are made of wood that you find in
the outdoors, but in some places, such as public
parks, one is required to use charcoal; in some
other places wood is not readily available, so charcoal is used, or wood is carried on the outing.
Since wood is the most common fuel, fire-lighting
with wood is described here.

Here are steps to take in learning to build a fire.
(See sections below for how-to-do-it.)

1. Fix a place for building the fire.
2. Learn the kinds of materials used in firebuilding, and gather a big handful of each
   (enough to keep the fire going three minutes—so you need not leave the fire, once
   it is lighted).
3. Build a *foundation* fire and
4. Keep it going and build into a *tepee* or *criss
   cross* fire, and use it to toast food.
5. As soon as you are through with it PUT IT
   OUT.

6. Unless you build in a ready-made fireplace, leave no trace of your fire.
7. Practice many times—in the wind, in the rain, etc. until you are sure you can light fires. (You may need to learn to light a match and let it get burning before you put it in the fire. Practice this, too.)
8. Try to have someone with you when lighting a fire. It is always safer this way than doing it alone.

STEP 1—FIXING A FIREPLACE

WHERE TO BUILD

—On sand, rocks or dirt. (NEVER at the base of a tree, or near enough for heat to kill the roots.) Ground should be cleared of leaves, grass, sticks, etc. down to solid dirt, over a large enough area, unless a stone fireplace is used. This is especially important in the woods. Clear away leaf mold, etc. to prevent fire from smoldering underground.

—In a fireplace, temporary or permanent. Temporary fireplaces are made of ditches or holes dug in dirt, green logs, rocks, bricks, clay or tin cans.

—With the wind at your back, as you face the fire. This will make a draft that blows *through* the fire when it is lighted.

STEP 2—MATERIALS TO USE

There are three types of material used in fires: *Tinder*, *kindling* and *fuel*.

TINDER: That material which catches fire from a match.

Should be in pieces not any thicker than a match, but longer. Shavings or fuzz sticks, fine twigs (especially from evergreen trees), bundles of tops of bushes or weeds, pieces of fat pine, thin pieces of bark, etc. make good tinder. (Paper, of course, but campcrafters scorn it except in great emergencies.) Beware of light material like grass or leaves; these flare up quickly, but have little real substance and burn out too quickly to catch on anything heavier.

KINDLING: Good dry sticks and twigs graduated in

size from pieces just bigger than tinder up to pieces as thick as a thumb, and from six to twelve inches long. Larger pieces may be split for kindling.

FUEL: The real fire material. Good firm pieces of wood, graduated in size from pieces just bigger than kindling up to good-sized logs, depending on use. Charcoal is often used as a fuel, too.

Learn each kind; be able to find some of each, and keep it handy in a good woodpile, either a small temporary one or a larger, more premanent one.

A good woodpile is a convenience, as well as a safety device. Stack wood so that tinder, kindling and fuel are in separate piles for convenience. Place woodpile near fireplace for convenience, but far enough away so you do not have to walk in it to get around the fire, and far enough away on the side away from the wind so sparks cannot possibly fly into it.

KINDS OF WOOD TO USE

You will probably be using whatever you find around when you first begin to light fires. As you progress, you will learn about certain types of wood, and which are best for certain purposes. Here are a few hints to help you make a woodpile that will be useful—

Wood for kindling should SNAP when broken. In general, dead branches from lower limbs of trees make the best kindling. Sticks lying on the ground may be damp.

Tinder may be anything that is very light and dry—not any thicker than a match. Make little bundles of tiny twigs.

Sticks that *bend* and do not snap are green; use only after a hot fire is started.

Wood that crumbles is rotten. (You'll find lots around—don't bother with it.) It has lost all its life and will just smoulder and smoke without giving off any heat.

Split wood burns well; the inside of a log is drier than the outside.

In wet weather, depend on dead branches on trees; they dry sooner than wood on the ground, as the air can get all around them.

SOFT WOOD is produced by trees that grow quickly—pines, spruces, cedars, gray birch, aspen, etc. This wood is good for starting fires, or for quick hot fires. It burns up quickly and needs constant refueling; it does not leave good coals.

HARD WOOD is produced by trees that grow slowly—oaks, hickories, yellow birch, maples, ash, mesquite, eucalyptus, etc. Hard wood is compact and firm, and feels heavy in the hand as compared with a piece of soft wood of the same size. This kind of wood burns slowly, and yields coals that will last. It needs a good hot fire to get started, and then burns well for a long time.

Visit a woodpile somewhere, and look over the wood there. Try picking up a few pieces, to see if you can tell which are *hard* and which are *soft*. Pick out some that will split for good kindling, some that will make good coals for broiling, some that will be good to burn in a fireplace on a cold day. What kinds of wood or other fuel are found around where you live?

STEP 3—START WITH A FOUNDATION FIRE

HOW TO BUILD A FOUNDATION FIRE

1. Have fireplace ready before you begin.

2. Have ready, at hand:
    —a big handful of tinder
    —a double handful of kindling
    —what fuel you will need, unless there are wood-gatherers working with you so you will not have to leave the fire after it is lighted.

3. Kneel with wind at your back; take two small sticks of kindling and place to form an angle in fireplace, as shown in Fig. 1; *or* place one stick across these two, to form an A.

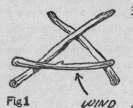

Fig 1   WIND

4. Pile a good bit of tinder in the angle of the sticks, or on cross piece, lightly, so there is air, but compactly enough so each piece rests against other pieces. Leave a tunnel at *center* and bottom in which to insert match. (Fig. 2)

LIGHT HERE

Fig 2

REMEMBER: Fire needs air.
           Flame burns *upward*.
           Only material in the path of flame will ignite.

Fig 3

5. Strike match, tipping down, so flame catches on wood. (Cup in hands, if necessary.) When well lighted, stick flame in air space, putting flame under the *center* of the pile of tinder. If match goes out, use it as extra tinder. Blow gently at *base* of fire, if necessary. (Fig. 3)

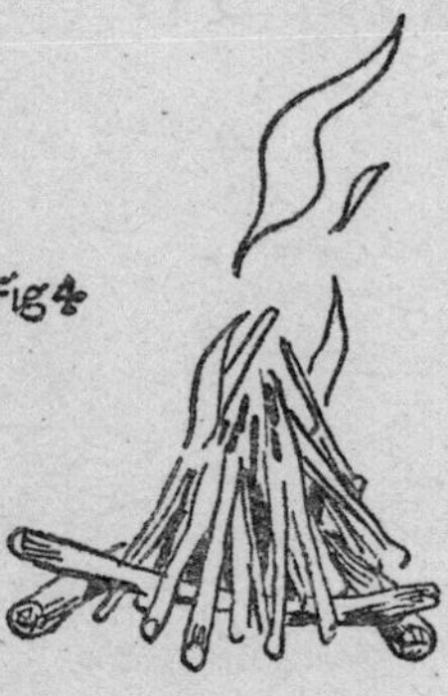

Fig 4

6. As flame catches and begins to spread, add bits of tinder, placing gently *on flame* until there is a brisk fire. (Fig. 4)

7. Then begin to add pieces of kindling, one by one, placing lightly where the flame is best, starting with small pieces, and gradually adding bigger pieces, forming a tepee shape. Do not make any *sudden* changes in size of wood used; add pieces that are just a bit larger than those already burning, until you are using thumb-sized sticks.

REMEMBER: Build gradually. Keep fire compact, each piece of wood touching other pieces for most of its length.

8. Put a small stick or poker in bottom of fire to raise just a little, to give more air.

9. When fire is going well, begin to add fuel in graduated sizes, building into the kind of a fire you will need.

STEP 4—BUILD INTO SOME TYPE OF FIRE

COOKING FIRES

Tepee or Wigwam Fire

A quick, hot fire for boiling, etc. Concentrates heat at a small point at top.

Start with a foundation fire. Continue building with fuel in tepee formation, as shown, keeping it tall, not widespread.

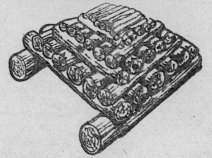

Crisscross Fire

A solid fire that will burn to coals, or produce a long-burning fire.

Start with foundation fire. Add fuel, as shown, to make a crisscross of sticks. Put thick sticks at bottom after foundation fire is going very well, lighter sticks across.

Reflector Fire

To provide high and steady heat for baking, planking, etc.

Start with a foundation fire, and build it into a high crisscross fire built against a rock or reflector of logs. Let it burn to good coals.

For quick browning, build a fire high against reflector, stones or logs.

AIR
SPACE

Trench Fire

To provide long, narrow fire for trench-type fireplace, start with one or more foundation fires, and when going well, knock flat, instead of building into tepee. Make a long, narrow crisscross type, with long sticks the length of firebox, and small sticks cross-wise, to provide air.

If fire seems to burn poorly, be sure you have plenty of air going in at the front. Raise sticks by a cross stick, if needed, in front.

Tin Can Fire

A small steady fire in a stove made of a tin can. (See page 96)

Start with a small fire of tinder. Have a supply of sticks no bigger than thumb (for a #10 stove). Keep fire small, and *feed steadily* with small twigs. Needs plenty of air; keep extra tinder handy for bolstering up!

Move can in place when fire is going. Tin can cookery needs two persons—one to cook, the other to feed fire.

Fire for Charcoal Stove—
(See page 97)

Make a small foundation fire—feed small twigs until there is a brisk fire. Then drop on small pieces of charcoal, gradually increasing size. Swing by the handle, or blow at base, to make fire burn.

CAMPFIRES

Campfires are generally laid some time before using, so the foundation fire must be sureproof, and the other structure in place before lighting.

Tepee type

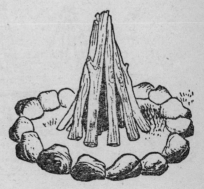

Crisscross-type fire

The trick is to be *sure* that there is *plenty of tinder and small kindling,* and a place to insert the first light. In ceremonials, it is better to use extra tinder than to have the fire lighting keep every one in a frenzy of anxiety!

Altar-type fire

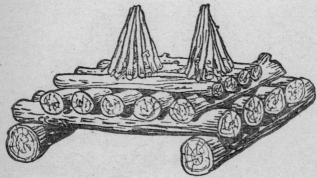

Altar-type fire

This is a special fire for ceremonials. Looks well in a fireplace, and is thrilling to watch burn. Goes against the old theory that fire burns up, but works if there is plenty of light stuff to ignite lower layers.

Make a long crisscross-type fire. On the top build one or two tepee fires, with leaders running down through the inside of the crisscrosses. Use *plenty* of tinder and small stuff, to make the rest catch.

Light the tepees, and fire will spread out and down until all is burning.

This type of fire should not need refueling through an evening.

Indoor fireplace fire

This may be a modification of either a tepee or a crisscross fire, generally built against a large back log.

Be sure there is enough small stuff and graduated sizes of wood to ignite the big logs. Once the fire is burning well, you can add logs. Keep the ashes in the bottom of fireplace; they conserve heat and help fill in air space.

Garbage disposal

Build a good, freely burning crisscross fire, and pile
garbage lightly on top.
Drain as much as possible
before hand, and add bit by
bit, not all at once. When
fuel is limited, dry garbage
in sun before burning.

It takes a GOOD FIRE to
burn garbage, which is generally very moist and needs
heat to dry out. Provide
plenty of air, too.

For a permanent garbage burning place, use a screening raised on stones or brick. Gives the fire room to burn
without being smothered.

When burning papers, bundle into hard balls to prevent them from blowing away when lighted. Tear paper
boxes into small pieces, and add gradually to fire.

STEP 5 — PUT IT OUT

As soon as you are through cooking, or whatever you are doing with the fire, begin to put it out. This is especially important if you are out for the day and must go away and leave the spot later.

(a) Let fire die down as much as possible.

(b) Scatter coals, break up big pieces, knock logs apart.

(c) Stir coals—and *sprinkle* with water—then stir again. Repeat until there are no live coals—under the logs or in the middle.

(d) If you have no water, put on sand or dirt, and stir thoroughly.

(e) When you can press your hand on the spot where the fire was, you know it is out.

(f) Cover with rocks or dirt—and check carefully before you leave.

FIRE SAFETY HINTS

Don't build fires when you are alone

Don't "play" with fire

Use fireplaces to enclose fires

Clear ground around fireplace so wind cannot blow a spark into leaves, grass, etc.

Dig a trench in ground if it is windy or if there are no stones or logs to enclose fire; pile dirt and sod to one side and replace when through

Build small fires

Break matches in two before throwing away
Never leave a fire unattended
Have some means for fighting fire on hand—
  pails of water, sand, etc.

IN CASE OF FIRE

You may take every precaution in building
your fire, yet a spark may jump out into the
leaves or grass and start a fire. You may come on
a small fire just starting from some carelessly-
thrown match as you hike through the woods.
Do something about it before it gets too large!
Here are some ways to take care of it:

—Send someone to notify fire wardens by tele-
  phone, unless you are SURE you can handle it.
  Keep cool, be deliberate.

—Use sand or dirt to smother flames, or use
  brooms, brush, burlap bags, or some other
  heavy material that can be soaked in water, to
  beat out the flames. If there are pails of water
  handy, make the water go further by this
  method, rather than trying to sprinkle on the
  flames. Use shovels to dig dirt to smother fire,
  or to dig a trench around it.

—Work with the wind IN YOUR FACE, not at
  your back. Beat toward the wind. (Beating
  with the wind at your back tends to help fan
  the flames, or causes sparks or flames to jump
  ahead into unburned area.)

—Larger fires require fire fighters and tools. An experienced man should organize that crew. Let the fire warden take charge, and help as he directs.

(Note: State and Federal Conservation Departments have excellent books to help with this. Write your state bureau of information to learn what is available.)

CHAPTER 6

Outdoor Food

"WHEN DO WE EAT?" and "WHAT'S FOR LUNCH?"—these are the big questions that go with any kind of outdoor fun, whether you are hiking for the day, having a picnic in the yard, or cooking for your unit at camp. Will it be sandwiches, hamburgers done to a turn, a stew, or reflector biscuits? OUTDOOR FOOD! It is very important, and the better the food, the better the campcrafting. Many different skills go into outdoor cooking: firebuilding and toolcraft as well as good planning and preparation. No one can claim to be a good campcrafter who is not a good camp cook.

Outdoor food does not always have to be cooked; a good hike lunch is part of the day when you want to cover lots of ground without taking the time to cook. For mountain climbing, lunches are often concentrated, with food that weighs little but is packed full of nourishment.

Outdoor food calls for a good bit of planning, packing, preparation and cleaning up—as well as that high point of eating! There are all sorts of good things to make, and many different types of cooking to try as you progress along the out-door cooking trail. Some of these one does for himself, some for the small group, and some for a large crowd. Whatever it is, you will be sure that it will be one of the best parts of the day when someone calls "Come and get it!" and you take that first bite.

Don't be too ambitious to begin with. Start with simple things, and when you have practiced them, progress to something else. Remember that the actual cooking is only a part of the job—making the fireplace, making the fire, and taking care of it will be more than half the job.

And don't think you cannot have a good cook-out unless you have steak or chicken. A good campcrafter can turn out a meal that costs very little, but that is sure to be tasty. In camp or at home, use leftovers and bits of this and that to make something really special. Don't stay at the frankfurter stage, either. Any one can cook a frankfurter (well, more or less!), and it *is* the great American picnic dish; but you won't be much of a campcrafter if you don't progress to other just-as-good and more-interesting-to-cook things.

Have some pride in how you cook! ANY ONE can burn a marshmallow, but not every one knows enough to toast one golden brown. (All right, burn it later if you like charcoal, but no camper will believe you can cook if you always burn the marshmallows or toast.)

In camp you will probably have a chance to talk over plans for cookouts with your tent or unit group. Try to cook out often, if it is possible, for you'll learn much campcrafting while you do. In camp it is fun to make a trail kitchen near your sleeping quarters, so it is easy to cook any meal. (See page 149)

In town you may have a place in your yard where you and your gang can fix up an outdoor fireplace and trail kitchen. Why not?—it will be a wonderful place to learn lots of campcrafting.

TYPES OF OUTDOOR FOOD

Here are some of the types of food, cooked or uncooked, that are part of outdoor fun. From your first hike lunch with nothing to cook, through the first steps in cooking, you can progress to the stage where all the parts of a meal are prepared on the trail or where you and your club stage a big meal, like a barbecue. If you do not know how to get started, try some things in this order:

Hike lunches—no cooking, but good planning, good packing

Lunches brought by each person, with one thing, like cocoa or soup, cooked for all

Something cooked for a group in a large frying pan—like hamburgers or eggs—to go with lunches brought by each person

Something cooked by each person in his own small frying pan—like bacon, a hamburger, an egg—to go with lunch brought all prepared

Something toasted on a stick—sandwiches, frankfurters, etc.

One-pot meals for a group—(a main dish all in one kettle)—like a stew

On-a-stick cooking (other than toasting)— such as bread twists, pioneer drumsticks

Reflector-oven baking

Tin-can cookery or on-a-rock cookery

Aluminum foil cookery

Planking—and other types of baking

Big affairs, like barbecues, imus, clambakes, beanholes, etc.

Remember that the fire makes the success of the cooking! Learn when to have a quick hot fire, when to have good coals, when to plan for a fire that burns for a long while. Firebuilding, the making of the fireplace, and cooking go hand in hand.

HIKE LUNCHES

Maybe the first thing you are going to do is to go on a hike with your class, your troop or club, each person bringing his own lunch. A camper will be able to tell at a glance that you are a campcrafter if you've packed a good lunch, plenty of it, but not too much—and when you open it, still good to eat! Take along the right amount, with an extra mid-afternoon snack, so you do not throw anything away or have anything to carry home. (These pointers are good for your school lunches, too.)

SANDWICHES—Take from two to five. Vary kinds of filling, and if possible, kinds of bread. Use some dark or enriched bread; for variety make one sandwich with one slice of white and one of dark bread.

—For fillings, have one sweet filling (jam), another meat (chopped ham), and a third, vegetable (lettuce). Moist fillings are better than dry. Spread fillings to edges of bread, rather than all in the middle. Buttering both pieces of bread prevents filling from soaking into bread. Substitutes for sandwiches: A roll stuffed with salad

A hard-boiled or deviled egg

A good-sized piece of cheese

A paper cup of salad (not too moist)

Crackers, rye crisp (watch out for fillings that make them soggy)

FRUIT—Fresh fruit, especially the kind that will quench thirst—oranges, apples, peaches, pears, tangerines or grapes.

—Dried fruit—raisins, prunes, apricots or figs. A generous handful makes a good portion.

RAW VEGETABLES—These help provide moisture and add freshness to the lunch. Carrots, scraped and cut in long strips, celery or radishes are good. Lettuce carries best if washed, dried and wrapped in wax paper, and inserted in the salad or sandwiches on the spot. Tomatoes carried whole, and sliced just before eating, prevent soggy sandwiches. A whole or half tomato to eat, as is, is a fine addition.

SOMETHING SWEET but not *too* sweet. Plain cake, cookies, a chocolate bar, maple sugar, a few nuts, or a few pieces of candy.

MILK, if possible; if it is hard to carry and to keep cool, have it before starting out, or on return, and depend on juicy fruit and a not-too-sweet lunch to relieve thirst. A fruit punch is refreshing if it can be kept cool, but it has lit-

tle food value, unless made with fresh fruit.
Tomato or fruit juices are good.

As for water—watch out for drinking it "just
anywhere"; take it with you if you are not
absolutely sure of the supply you may want to
use on the hike. (See page 14)

AVOID FOODS THAT

—*Are sticky, or will get soft in heat, like mo-
lasses candy, or chocolate in extreme heat.*

—*Are very rich or soft, like some frostings.*

—*Are apt to get soggy, as pie or crackers with
cheese spread.*

—*Do not "carry" well in pocket or pack, like
cream puffs or lemon meringue pie.*

—*Have little food value, compared to their size
or weight, like fresh grapefruit or bottled
drinks.*

—*Will taste flat when warm, like bottled
drinks.*

PACKING HIKE LUNCHES

When you have decided what to have, give a
thought to the wrapping and packing. Waxed
paper and paper napkins are great boons to hike
lunches. A bread wrapper makes a good lunch
wrapping.

Pack lunches in individual small boxes like
candy boxes (preferably cardboard) or in paper
bags. These can then be burned after lunch and
need not be carried back.

In camp, lunches are often packed as "nose-bag" or "poke" lunches, meaning that the lunch for one person is placed in a bag, and carried by the person in a bandana, or tied to the belt.

In packing, use plenty of waxed paper. Pack heaviest items in bottom of bag. Wedge paper napkins in between them, so there is no room for shifting. Prepare vegetables beforehand, and wrap in waxed paper. Tie package securely, leaving a loop of string to tie to belt, or tie in bandana, hobo style.

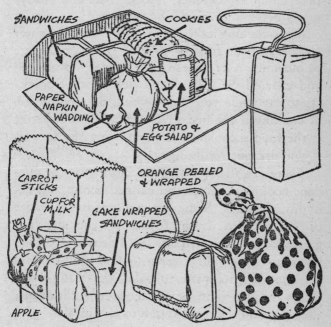

WHEN YOU COOK OUT

The things that you plan for an outdoor meal are very much like those you have at home, as far as need for planning a good, well-balanced and attractive meal goes. But some things are more fun to cook outdoors. You may plan extra amounts because you'll be hungrier, and the fuel you have or the place for cooking may make a difference in what you can plan. If you are just learning, plan only one thing to be cooked, and take along sandwiches, juices, fruit and ready-made desserts to round out the meal.

Most cooking takes time—time for the water to boil and the food to cook or time for the fire to burn down to coals so your food is not smoked and charred. So plan a sandwich or some crackers to eat while you wait—you'll do a better job of cooking if the fire is right; you'll like it better if the food is cooked well; and it is easier to wait if you are not *too* hungry!

There are all sorts of good short cuts for outdoor cooking—mixes and canned things and dehydrated foods. Some canned goods are easier to carry than fresh foods, if you are not going too far; concentrated and dehydrated food like soups are good for carrying and good for eating too. If you want to bake, the ready-made mixes are just right. Learn to use reflector ovens; they can add the right touch to any meal.

PLANNING MENUS

Simple meals are best. Choose the main item that is to be cooked, and plan the rest of the meal around that. That is, if you have a heavy dessert, plan a light main dish; if you have a good one-pot stew, plan a fruit dessert. To be sure you have a well-balanced meal, follow this plan:

For *one meal*, include:

An egg, meat, fish, or piece of cheese
Milk, if possible (for drinking and cooking)
Fruit of some kind
At least one vegetable (except for breakfast)
Dark or enriched bread

In the meals *for a day*, include:

At least a pint of milk (for drinking and cooking.) Carry canned or powdered or pasteurized milk—don't pick up milk from any farm along the road.
Fruit of some kind, twice
Cereals or bread, dark or enriched
Two or more vegetables, one of which should be green, leafy, or uncooked
A potato, in addition to other vegetable
A small portion of meat, cheese, fish, egg, dried beans or peas
Butter or fortified margarine

GENERAL SUGGESTIONS FOR MEALS

BREAKFAST: Fresh or cooked fruit
Hot or cold cereal
Pancakes or bacon or eggs - OR
Toast and bacon or eggs - OR
French toast or biscuits
Honey, jam or syrup as needed
Cocoa or milk

DINNER: Meat, fish, eggs or cheese
Vegetables, one cooked, one raw
Rice, potatoes, macaroni, noodles
or spaghetti
Dessert to balance; use fruit with
a heavy meal; plan a light meal
if you want to cook short-
cake or doughboys
Milk

LUNCH OR (Plan this with heavier meal of
SUPPER: day in mind; make it light if
dinner has been or will be
heavy.)
One-pot dishes, salads, and sand-
wiches, individual stick cook-
ing, soups
Raw vegetable or salad
Bread and butter or toast or bis-
cuits
Dessert, as for dinner
Milk or cocoa

TYPES OF OUTDOOR COOKING

Here are various types of cooking, and little helps to make these successful.

TOASTING—"to brown by heat." Best done over good coals; patience in waiting for the fire to burn to coals is its own reward! A good campcrafter toasts his bread or marshmallows *golden brown,* evenly done on all sides. He doesn't say he "likes it burned" just because he is not skillful enough to do a good job.
When a flaming fire must be used, hold the food to one side of the flames, instead of *in* or *over* them, or the food will be smoked instead of toasted.

BROILING—"to cook by direct exposure to heat." Broiling is a method used in cooking meat, especially tender cuts like chops or steak. It is usually done on a green stick, a green stick broiler, or on a wire rack or broiler. Broiling is best done over coals; the food should be turned often and cooked slowly. As in toasting, flames will smoke the food.

PAN BROILING is done in a pan (usually for meat). Heat the pan first, put in meat, turn often, pouring off fat as it accumulates, keeping as dry as possible so meat does not fry.

STEWING OR BOILING—"to cook in water." Tougher cuts of meat are

BOILING

good for stew; they have more flavor, but take longer to cook. For stews, meat should be browned quickly in fat, and cooked slowly in water until tender. Generally speaking, the longer the cooking, the better the stew.

For boiling, have a cover on the pot to hasten the process; put the kettle on the fire as soon as it is going to catch all the heat.

TIN-CAN FRYING

FRYING—"to brown or sear in fat in a pan." Best done over a bed of coals, since flames are likely to lick into the pan. Generally, a small amount of fat is all that is necessary for frying. Draining fried foods on a paper napkin helps to get rid of excess grease.

When frying bacon, onions, etc., for a one-pot meal, fry in the bottom of the kettle to be used, and pour off the grease when brown, adding other ingredients as needed.

TIN CAN STOVES—often used for frying.

ON-A-ROCK

ON-A-ROCK COOKING is another kind of frying in which a flat stone is heated and used as a frying pan.

CLAM BAKE

STEAMING is cooking by steam. Little or no additional moisture is added to the food, so it cooks in its own natural juices. Double boilers are used to cook or warm food; improvised "pressure cookers" may be made. Aluminum foil cooking is a steam process, as are imus and clambakes.

BAKING—there are many ways of baking out of doors. One way is on the end of a green stick, as you do for a bread twist; this is a slower process than toasting, for the outside must not get cooked too quickly, or the inside will not be cooked.

Another way is in reflector ovens; they may be made from tin cans. Dutch ovens are also used for baking.

PLANKING is the art of cooking on a board, generally by reflected heat. It is used for meat and fish.

NON-UTENSIL MEALS are those where you use no kettles or pans, but make any implements you need, like broilers or toasting sticks. This is a fine campcrafting kind of meal. Your jackknife is your best friend here!

ONE-POT MEALS are those where many ingredients make the main dish, like a chowder or stew. Everything is prepared in one kettle, and one needs only fruit or sweets to top off the meal.

BEANHOLES, IMUS AND CLAMBAKES are "fireless cookers" in the ground. (An imu is a Hawaiian way of cooking meat.)

BARBECUES are ways of roasting large pieces of meat over coals; a special sauce is used for basting the meat.

STEPS IN OUTDOOR COOKING

Suggestions for the SIMPLEST THINGS to toast that might be included in lunches:

Sandwiches to be toasted—
Cheese, meat, jelly, raisin bread

Bread to be toasted; make the sandwiches on the spot

Rolls spread with cheese spread, or just split and toasted

Frankfurters

Desserts—Marshmallows
* Marguerites
* Some-mores

Suggestions for things to cook on a green stick, or a green stick broiler:

Foods listed above

Steak, bacon or ham, chops, etc.

* Bread twists
* Pioneer drumsticks
* Kebabs
Desserts—* Lots-mores

Suggestions for One-Pot Dishes:
* Chili Con Carne
* Chowder
* Campfire Stew
* American Chop Suey
* Savory Beans

Desserts cooked in a pot—
* Chocolate Drops
* Candied Apples

FRANKFURTER IN A BREAD TWIST

Suggestions for Things to Bake:

In a Reflector Oven—
Ginger Cookies
Cornflake Macaroons
Corn Bread
Biscuits

Suggestions for things to cook in individual small frying pans (6-inch pan costs about $.20), or on a tin can stove or a hot rock:

Anything that can be fried
Hamburgers
Frankfurters
Bacon (better to *start* this way than over an open fire on a stick)
Eggs—fried or scrambled
Sandwiches, like cheese dreams
*Pancakes
Ham slices; try prepared ham for economy
Apple and sausages
Fish, meat or potato cakes
Chops, small pieces of meat like cube steak
*Scrambled potatoes

Baked in the coals—
Potatoes
*Potatoes in tin cans
*Fish in a bag
*Roast Corn
Little Pig Potatoes

In a Beanhole—
Stews
Ham slices
Baked beans
Cooked cereal

On a plank—
Fish
Steak
Chops
Liver

Suggestions for Beverages:
*Cocoa
*Coffee
Tea

(Recipes of items * starred are on pages 74-91.)

USING WHAT IS LEFT OVER
OR ON HAND

Often you can cook out, at home or in camp, if you do not need something special. Your mother or the camp dietitian may have some fine little tidbits that will just fit into your plan— see what you can make of what is in the refrigerator.

HAMBURG OR CHOPPED MEAT
fry or broil
* pioneer drumsticks
* in almost any one-pot meal that calls for meat

FRANKFURTERS
broil, boil or fry
cook in bread twist
cooked—cut in pieces, and used in one-pot dishes, pea soup or potato salad

FLOUR
* pancakes
* bread twists
biscuits, cornbread, gingerbread cookies, etc. in a reflector or tin can oven

LEFT-OVER COOKED MEAT OR CANNED MEAT OR FISH
cold sliced
chopped or sliced, in sandwiches
chopped or cubed, in salads
in one-pot dishes or chowders
chopped, in stuffed peppers or hash or meat cakes
* chowder

CANNED MILK
* in cocoa or eggnog
in soups or chowders
in puddings
in pancakes, etc.
anywhere whole milk is used

RICE OR SPAGHETTI
  as a vegetable instead of potato
  in soups and one-pot meals
  rice in puddings
    with raisins or dates as dessert
  rice in pancakes or meat cakes

BACON
  broil or fry
  cooked—cut in pieces and used in scrambled eggs, sandwiches, chowders, one-pot dishes
  in club sandwiches, with tomato, toast, etc.

SUGAR
  fudge
  *chocolate drops
  *candied apples

LEFT-OVER COOKED VEGETABLES
Potatoes:
  fry or cream
  with egg, meat, bacon, etc. in salads
  *scrambled potatoes
  mashed—in meat or potato cakes or hash
Other vegetables:
  in salads
  in one-pot dishes
  in soups

EGGS
  fried, boiled, scrambled, etc.
  baked in orange skins or potatoes
  hard boiled—in sandwiches, or plain, or stuffed, or in salads
  cold scrambled eggs make good sandwich filling
  *scrambled potatoes

(A good campcrafter is always making up new recipes—generally because of what is left over!)

(Recipes of items *starred are on pages 74-76, 78-88, 90-91.)

◇◇◇

BASIC RECIPES

◇◇◇

(Serves 8)   (Frying pan)
BASIC PANCAKE RECIPE

3 cups flour
1 teaspoon salt
1½ tablespoons baking
  powder
1 or 2 eggs
2 cups milk
2 tablespoons melted fat
Grease for frying

Frying pan—individual
  ones are good (or tin
  can stoves)
Turners
Bowl or pan
Spoon

Mix dry ingredients, add eggs slightly beaten, then milk gradually, last of all melted fat. Batter should just pour from spoon.

Have pan hot and well greased. Pour spoonful on pan, cook until bubbles appear on top, then turn. The smaller, the easier for beginners to cook. Try flipping, using individual pans. When using batter for a large group, give each camper a paper cup of batter.

Variation: Add 2 cups blueberries or cooked rice, or 2 teaspoons cinnamon and 2 tablespoons sugar.

———

(Per person)   (On-a-stick)
BREAD TWISTS OR DOUGHBOYS

1/2 cup flour
1 teaspoon baking powder   or 3/4 of a cup prepared biscuit flour
1 teaspoon shortening
Pinch of salt
About 1/4 cup water
Small amount of extra flour

Green stick, one end a little bigger than thumb; peeled 3 inches down
Cup or small paper bag
Coals

Mix dry ingredients in bag or cup; work in shortening with fingers. Add water slowly, until stiff dough is formed. Handle as little as possible to keep from getting tough. Make it stiff enough to hold together; add a little flour if it gets too moist. (Only practice will tell you!)

Heat stick; flour it; flour hands; put half mixture on stick, winding like a ribbon spirally down the stick, with space between twists, OR place over the end, squeezing gently into a long thin covering. Cook by holding about six inches away from coals at first, so inside will bake, then brown nearer coals. Turn continually. Will slip off stick easily when done. Stuff hole with bacon, jam, etc.

(Per person)   (One-pot)

BASIC CHOWDER RECIPE

1 slice fat bacon or 1   Kettle
   small square salt pork   Jackknife
1/8 onion per person   Ladle or spoon
1/2 medium-sized potato
   (diced)
1/4 can corn, 1/4 pound
   fish, etc.
Salt and pepper
1 cup liquid (water,
   stock or milk)

Cut bacon or pork and onions very small. Fry in bottom of kettle until brown. (Stir frequently to prevent burning. Pour off extra grease, if necessary.)

Add corn, fish or meat, with a little water, as needed. Let cook slowly until fish or meat is cooked. Add diced potatoes about 1/2 hour before time for serving and cook until done. Season, and add milk just before serving, if using milk. Bring to boiling point, but do not boil.

(Serves 8)   (One-pot)

CREAM SAUCE

8 tablespoons butter or   Kettle or double boiler
  oleo or bacon drippings   Spoon
8 tablespoons (½ cup)
  flour   *Slow fire*
1 teaspoon salt
4 cups milk

Melt butter (or other fat) in bottom of kettle; add flour, stirring well until smooth paste is formed and mixture bubbles vigorously. Add cold milk, heat, stirring constantly until thick and smooth.

Beginners may use double boiler made by two kettles, one inside the other; put boiling water in outside kettle.

(Some experts say you cannot really cook outdoors until you can make a GOOD cream sauce over an open fire!)

(Serves 8)   (One-pot)

AMERICAN CHOP SUEY

2 cans spaghetti with to-
  mato sauce

2 teaspoons fat

3-4 onions (small), peeled
  and diced

1-1½ pounds hamburg
  steak

Green pepper if desired,
  cut small

Salt and pepper

Frying pan or kettle
Jackknife

Fry onions and pepper in fat until brown. Pour
off excess fat. Add hamburg steak, and cook until
well done, but not crisply brown. Add spaghetti
and heat well. Season to taste. Serve hot.

Instead of canned spaghetti, use 1 package
macaroni and 1 can concentrated tomato soup.
Cook macaroni in boiling water. Takes an extra
kettle.

For variety: Use a little sausage meat with the
        hamburg; add some cooked celery.

———————

(Serves 8)   (One-pot)
SCRAMBLED POTATOES

8 medium-sized cold   Jackknives
   boiled potatoes, diced   Frying pan or kettle
2 small onions, peeled and
   diced
4 pieces bacon, cut in small
   pieces, or small amount
   bacon fat
8 eggs
Salt and pepper

Fry onions with bacon pieces, or in bacon fat until light brown. Add potatoes, and fry until
brown and crisp. Break eggs into mixture, stirring while it cooks; cook until eggs are set. Season well. Serve hot.

Add a little cheese or tomato catsup or both, if
desired.

———————

(Serves 8)   (One-pot)
CHILE CON CARNE

4 tablespoons drippings   Kettle
About 8 tablespoons   Spoon
   chopped onion   Jackknife
1½-2 pounds ground steak
   or left-over meat
2 quarts canned tomatoes
2 cans kidney beans
Salt

Fry onion in fat until light brown. Add meat, and cook until done. Add tomatoes and beans, and cook together. Season with chili powder and salt. Let it all simmer. Thicken with a little flour if needed. Add 2 tablespoons of Worcestershire sauce, if more seasoning is needed.

Note: You may want to add a little chili powder. Add it carefully.

(Serves 8)   (One-pot)

CAMPFIRE STEW

1½-2 pounds hamburg steak   Kettle or frying pan

3 teaspoons fat   Jackknife

1 large onion, peeled and diced   Spoon

2 cans CONCEN-TRATED vegetable soup

Salt and pepper

Make little balls of hamburg, adding seasoning. Fry with onions in frying pan, or in bottom of kettle, until onion is light brown and balls are well browned all over. Pour off excess fat. Add vegetable soup and enough water or soup stock to prevent sticking. Cover, and cook slowly until meat balls are cooked all through. (The longer, the better.)

(Serves 8)   (One-pot)
SAVORY BEANS

6 frankfurters or sausages,   Kettle
  or 1 lb. sausage meat   Spoon
1 can or 2 cups cooked   Jackknife
  corn kernels
2 cans or 4 cups baked
  beans
1 medium-sized onion,
  peeled and chopped
  fine

Cut sausages in small pieces (or make small balls of meat), and fry with onion until brown. Pour off any excess fat.

Add corn and beans. Add a little water, if needed. Season to taste, and heat well, stirring to prevent sticking.

Add a little catsup if desired. Serve HOT.

(Per person)   (One-pot)
POCKET STEW
Each person brings a handful of cleaned and cut up vegetables, meat, etc. in a piece of waxed paper.

Fry onions (if any) and bacon together in pot; add a little water and any meat and vegetables; simmer slowly until done. (A few bouillon cubes help to give a good flavor.)

BEVERAGES

COCOA

1 teaspoon cocoa   Kettle
2 teaspoons sugar
1 cup milk, or equivalent:
   ½ cup evaporated milk
   and ½ cup water; *or* 4
   tablespoons milk pow-
   der and 1 cup water
A little extra water

Mix cocoa and sugar with water in kettle, and
cook to a smooth paste, letting it bubble vigorously. Add milk and stir all thoroughly together.

Heat almost to a boil. Some add a pinch of salt. Beating with a whip prevents any scum from forming.

———————

(Per person)   Beverage
COFFEE

1 cup water per person   Coffee pot
1 HEAPING tablespoon   Bag of cheesecloth
  coffee (regular grind)   and string
1 extra tablespoon coffee
  for every 10 cups
  (1 lb. coffee makes 45
  cups)

Cold water coffee: Put coffee in bag, place bag in the water in pot, put on fire and bring to a boil. Boil 3 minutes for ordinary strength, longer for stronger. Remove bag; keep *hot.*

The bag just makes it easier to clean pot. Be sure the bag is large enough to allow coffee to swell. A large square of cheesecloth caught up at the corners does just as well as a bag.

Boiling water coffee: Bring water to a boil, then add the bag of coffee and boil 3 to 4 minutes. (Some think this has the advantage of fresher tasting coffee, since coffee has not soaked in water.)

Without the bag: Use the same proportions, and clear with egg shells or cold water when cooked.

(Per person)   (Non-Utensil)

FISH IN A BAG

1/4-1/3 lb. solid white fish per person (cod, haddock or any fillet is good)
Salt and pepper
Lemon butter (3 tablespoons melted butter with 1 tablespoon lemon juice) *or* a small piece of butter

Heavy wax paper
Newspaper or small paper bags

Good bed of coals

Place piece of fish in a good-sized piece of wax paper; salt and pepper it, and add lemon butter or piece of butter. Wrap wax paper around fish, turning it on all sides. Then wrap well in bag or newspaper that has been soaked in water.

Have a good bed of coals ready, and place the packet on top of the coals; leave for about 20-30 minutes, depending on size of fish, turning once. If paper becomes too dry, remove from fire and wet again; then return to coals. It cooks by steaming.

———————

(Per person)   (Non-Utensil)
ROAST CORN

2-3 ears of green corn   String
Salt and pepper   GOOD *bed of coals*
Butter   Wire screening over coals
         for large number

Peel ears, leaving husks on at bottom, and remove corn silk. Then replace husks, covering ears, and tie around top. (Some people dip corn in salt water at this point.)

Have a good bed of coals in trench or round fireplace, and place screening across logs or stones, just above coals. Place ears on screening. Turn often, until all sides are done. Strip ears, leaving husk on the end for a handle; add salt, pepper, and butter to taste. Eat immediately. May also be done by standing ears upright at sides of fireplace, turning often. If you like the kernels brown, strip ears after they have steamed awhile, and finish cooking by direct exposure to heat, turning as above.

◇◇◇

STICK COOKERY

◇◇◇

(8 persons)   **(On-a-stick)**

PIONEER DRUMSTICKS

2 lbs. chopped beef
1 cup cornflakes, crumbled
   fine
2 eggs (optional)
Pepper, onion, salt, if
   desired
16 rolls or slices of bread

8 green sticks about the
size of thumb. Peel thick
end 3 inches

Mix beef, seasonings, eggs and cornflakes together thoroughly. Make 16 portions.

Wrap a portion around end of a stick, squeezing in place evenly. Make it long and thin, not a ball. Be sure there are no air spaces in it. (Watch out for big pieces of cornflake.)

Cook slowly over coals, turning frequently so all sides are evenly cooked. Twist slightly to take off stick. Serve in roll. Some prefer to roll the meat in crumbled cornflakes after placing it on the stick to make a crust. Try it both ways!

———

(Per person)   **(On-a-stick)**

KEBABS

¼ lb. round steak cut in small pieces, trimmed of fat, about 1 inch square by ¼ inch thick

Small onion peeled and cut in slices

Partially boiled potato, if desired, sliced ¼ inch thick

2 strips bacon, cut in squares

2 rolls or sandwiches

Pointed green sticks about size of little finger; peel down three inches

Jackknife

Coals

Place pieces of steak, onion, bacon and potato alternately on sticks, pushing them down the stick and leaving a little space between pieces. Repeat in same order.

Sear quickly all over by holding close to coals, then cook slowly a little away from coals, turning until done.

For OYSTER BABS—use oysters and pieces of bacon.

For LIVER BABS—use small pieces of liver and pieces of bacon.

◇◇

DESSERTS

◇◇

(Serves 8)   Dessert (on-a-stick)
SOME-MORES

16 marshmallows (about ½ lb.)

32 graham crackers (about 1 large pkg.)

6-5-cent chocolate bars, the flat kind without nuts (break in thirds)

Green sticks for toasting
Jackknives

Coals

Make a sandwich of a piece of chocolate and two crackers. Toast a marshmallow golden brown, and well puffed. (SLOWLY over coals does it!) Pop into the sandwich; press gently together, and eat. Tastes like "some more."

Variations: Use peanut butter instead of chocolate—"Robinson Crusoes." Use slices of apples instead of crackers—"apple some-mores." Use chocolate-covered crackers instead of chocolate bars. Use a chocolate peppermint instead of milk chocolate.

———

(Per person)   Dessert (on-a-stick)
MARGUERITES

2 marshmallows   Green sticks, split on thick
2 soda crackers   end, about 3 inches
2 nut meats (walnuts,   down
  pecans or large
  peanuts)   *Coal or reflector oven*

Place a marshmallow on top of a soda cracker, and a nut meat on top of the marshmallow. Place all in the split green stick, and toast. Toast cracker side first, then marshmallow side. (May be baked in a reflector oven.)

Note: Good way to use stale soda crackers!

———

(Per person)   Dessert (on-a-stick)
LOTS-MORES

3 marshmallows   Split green stick
3 squares milk chocolate Jackknife
  (as marked on five-cent
  bar)   *Coals*

Split marshmallow through middle. Insert square of chocolate. Put in split stick and toast. When marshmallow is toasted, chocolate will be melted inside.

(Serves 8)   Dessert
CANDIED APPLES

1½ lbs. sugar   Kettle
6 tablespoons butter   Pointed sticks about 6
1 small can corn syrup   inches long
8 good-sized apples   Spoon
Water in cup to test   Cup

Cook sugar, butter and syrup in kettle, stirring
constantly. When syrup seems to pour heavily
from spoon, test in cup of water, cooking until a
small amount hardens in water.

Remove from fire, and put apple on stick, and
dip so that the apple is well coated with syrup.
Twirl in air until cool. If syrup seems to harden
before all apples are dipped, heat again, or keep
kettle in another kettle of hot water while dip-
ping.

Keep hands away from drips—HOT!

———————

(Serves 8)   Dessert
CHOCOLATE DROPS

1 cup sugar   Small kettle
⅛ cup cocoa   Spoon
½ cup milk   Small sticks
16-24 marshmallows   Pieces of wax paper
                                 3-inch square
                             Cup of water

Make a fudge of sugar, cocoa and milk, stirring
enough to keep from sticking. When fudge is
cooked enough to make a soft ball in a cup of

water, remove from fire. Place marshmallows on sticks, and dip into fudge, turning until well covered, but not too long. Twist in air, using wax paper squares to catch the drips. Eat when cool. The second round will be cooler, and will form a hard coating of fudge on the marshmallow.

Variation: Make brown sugar fudge.

BAKING

(Serves 8)   (Baking)
POTATOES BAKED IN TIN CAN

8 medium-sized potatoes   2-# tin cans, with wire
                               handles (punch holes on
                               opposite sides of can
                               near top to insert wire
                               handle)
                               Heavy wax paper
Good bed of coals   Sand or dirt

Scrub potatoes well, and wrap each in wax paper. Put a layer of sand or dirt in bottom of a can; then put in potatoes with sand or dirt in between so no potato touches another potato or sides of the can. Pack sand or dirt well around the potatoes, and cover well. Wet the sand or dirt until a bit of it holds its shape when squeezed.

Have a good hot bed of coals ready, and place the cans directly in the coals, piling coals around the sides. Leave for about an hour, keeping coals raked around the cans. (Time varies a little with size of potatoes. When the ones on top are done, they are all done.) Moisten sand occasionally if it becomes too dry, adding water with a cup.

FOR BAKING WITH REFLECTOR OVEN

For beginners: Try small objects like cookies, rather than whole cakes. Gingerbread mix is especially good.

Try any cookie or drop cake recipe or a ready-packed mix; recipe on box.

Make cinnamon rolls or prepared biscuits.

Marguerites (see recipes) are good in a reflector oven.

NEXT STEP IN BAKING—DUTCH OVEN COOKING

CAMP COOKING HELPS

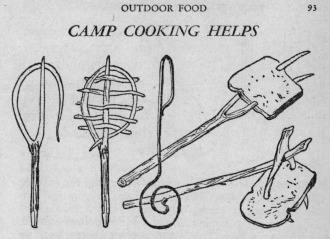

Broilers and sticks for toasting

Pot hooks and holders

A cooking paddle—Make a wooden paddle for stirring stews, cocoa, or soup. Make long enough to extend outside your largest kettle, or make several sizes. Can be made from scrap lumber. Make a broad bottom surface, sandpaper smooth. The broad surface covers more of the bottom of the kettle, and is more useful than a pointed spoon.

A whip from a green twig; a bandana for a pot holder or a handy towel on your belt; a "table" near the fireplace for spoon or paddle; smear soap on the outside of kettles—for easier cleaning.

WIND

Fix your trench fireplace so that your kettles or pans rest easily without someone having to hold them. Cook with the wind at your back. Put kettle on as soon as you start the fire.

A round fireplace is good for toasting or broiling by several people at a time, or for a Dutch oven.

For reflector baking, build against a high back of rocks or logs; a wire screening over coals is good for roasting corn.

Cut door; punch holes in opposite sides for draft; heat top grease and wipe off; then grease again and fry on top.

A VAGABOND STOVE conserves fuel. May be made from #10 cans, or from larger cracker or shortening tins.

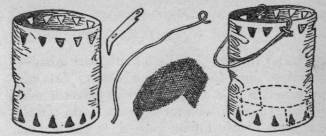

A charcoal stove—Make from a #10 (or larger) can. Put holes in bottom and top with punch opener; put on a handle of wire. Put a piece of screening in bottom to keep charcoal bits from falling out.

Aluminum Foil Cookery is a new "trick" in outdoor cooking. You need a fire of coals—not too hot—for this. Wrap the food carefully in the foil, with all seasoning inside; turn edges so that no steam can escape, folding over twice at each edge, and leaving air space inside. For example— a hamburg patty with onions, celery, carrot, tomato catsup—all wrapped together. Place this on top of coals, and leave for five to ten minutes, depending on what is inside.

YOUR OWN COOKING KIT

Perhaps you have a cooking kit that has a frying pan, small kettle, plate, cup, and so forth, with its own cover. This is a good start in the way of having your own equipment. Make one, if you do not have one; a small frying pan, an enamel or plastic plate and cup, and a tin can kettle make a fine one. Make a hike kit for it, too.

GROUP COOKING KITS

One of the best things is a kettle with a bail— a nest of such kettles is even better. You can make kettles from tin cans. A pack basket is good for carrying the food for a group. Begin to collect your own camping gear—it is much more fun when you have everything handy. (See page 21.)

PACKING FOODS

Pack baskets, knapsacks, or kettles are generally used to carry food for outdoor meals. Kettles with handles on them can easily be used as containers.

Pack heaviest things in the bottom of baskets or kettles. Pack so that there is no room for the various articles to shift around.

Wrap eggs in paper napkins, or carry them in an egg carton, or put them in the bag of flour to carry them safely.

Waterproofed cotton bags are excellent for carrying dry food. A good campcrafter will make his own.

CHAPTER 7

Knot Craft

EVER break your shoestring? Ever wanted to put up a line for drying your wet clothes? Ever tried to tie up a blanket roll? Ever tried to hitch a boat or a horse? You needed a knot— and the right one. Knots are an important part of a campcrafter's equipment, and with a good rope in his knapsack and the know-how in his head and fingers, a campcrafter will find knots as useful in camp as a sailor does on a ship. Besides, there are many skills and crafts that are based on knot tying.

There are hundreds of knots, each made just so, each for a specific use. Learn a few to begin with, and others will be easy to learn. The history of knots and the story of rope-making are both fascinating. There are many books about knots and knot tying to give you more than the glimpse given here.

Knot tying is a general term used for the making of bends, hitches, knots, slings, splices and lashings—all methods of tying rope or cord. Certain knots are used for certain purposes; there are several types of knots, and it is important to learn WHY you tie a certain knot while you are learning to tie it. Here are some types:

—Knots used for *joining* ropes or cord or string
—*Stopper* or *end* knots, to keep ropes from slipping through a hole or ring, or to keep the end from raveling
—*Loop* knots, providing a loop in the rope
—Hitches for *securing* rope, to make "fast"
—Knots for *shortening* rope
—Slings for *holding* articles

A *good* knot is one that can be TIED EASILY, WILL HOLD FAST, WILL NOT JAM, and can be UNTIED EASILY. Your own invention of several knots one on top of another may hold, but it probably doesn't qualify for the last test of a good knot. A thrifty camper does not cut a good piece of rope; he uses a knot, and later uses the rope again.

Start by learning one knot of each type, and you'll have a good set of knot tricks in your campcraft knapsack. Here's how to start—

1. Get a piece of clothesline or small rope about *four feet long*.

2. Look at the pictures, and follow step by step —or get someone who knows how to teach you.

3. When you can tie from the pictures, try the knot out on a chair, a tree, a box, or however it is supposed to be used.

4. Try to catch the *feel* of the knot—learn how it *looks* when it is right.

5. Practice—and practice! Do it with your eyes shut, or behind your back!

6. Find ways in your everyday life to use knots—there are lots of times when just the right knot helps the situation.

WHIPPING A ROPE

When the end of the rope keeps fraying, there is a way to stop it—"whip" it. This makes it look better, keeps the rope intact, and makes it easier to handle.

The simplest ways to stop raveling temporarily are:

1. Wrap a small strip of adhesive tape or scotch tape around the end, or

2. tie a small piece of string tightly around the end, or

3. make an overhand knot, if rope is small.

The campcraft way to do it is to "whip" it, for a permanent end. You'll need:

Your rope

A piece of string about 12 inches long

Make a loop of one to two inches with one end of the string (A), and place it on the end of rope, so that it lies along the rope. The short end of cord (B) and the long end (C) should hang off the rope's end. Hold loop of string on rope with one thumb and forefinger, so loop A is on top of rope, and ends hang off end. (Fig. 1)

Holding thumb near end of rope, start winding cord (C) *back down the length of rope,* away from the end, being sure to leave the short end (B) hanging off the end of the rope.   (Fig. 2)

As you wind neatly and tightly away from end, be sure to catch the string under your winding, letting your thumb slip back as you secure it, winding toward loop A, but not covering it.

When you have wound about ¾ of an inch, stop winding, and tuck the end (C) with which you have been winding, into the loop (A) and pull (C) taut.   (Fig. 3)

The short end of cord (B) should be still hanging off the end of the rope. Now pull this end (B), and you will discover that the loop (A) with the other end of cord (C) is slowly disappearing under the winding. Pull until you figure that the loop is about halfway down under the winding (Fig. 4), and then cut off both ends of cord, close to winding.

Now try to push the whipping off. If you can't, that's a good one; if you can, try again, winding the string more tightly.

And now to knots—here are just a few of some of the types mentioned above:

SQUARE KNOT

This is used for *joining* two ends of rope, cord or string of approximately the same size or thickness. Use it to tie up a bundle, a bandage, a broken shoestring, or to make a longer rope from several short ones.

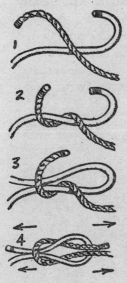

Take one end of each rope, one in either hand.
Cross the end in the right hand over the end in the left hand (Fig. 1), twisting it back, down and up in front, so that you make a single knot, and the end you started with is now in your left hand.   (Fig. 2)

Now take the end that is in your right hand and bend it over to the left so that it makes a loop and lies along the knot already made.   (Fig. 3)

Look closely and you will see that there is only one place for the other end (now in your left hand) to go, and that is into the loop you have made.   (Fig. 4)

TO LOOSEN PUSH

Take hold of the knot on both sides, and tighten by pulling the ends in opposite directions (Fig. 4). To loosen the knot, take hold in the same way, and push toward the center of the knot.   (Fig. 5)

5

Look at the knot: Does it look "square"? Each piece of rope should double back and lie alongside of itself, going in and coming out.

(If you are left-handed, just reverse the process —it doesn't matter.)

BEWARE of a "granny" knot—made by those who don't know how. It is a square knot gone wrong—won't hold, looks wrong.

You will notice that the square knot is for joining ropes of the *same* thickness. What about two ropes of different sizes? The *sheet bend* does that; it is the square knot with an extra twist in it, making sure it will hold fast.

SHEET BEND

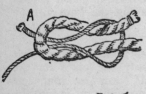

A

FIG. 1

Make a square knot in the ends of the two ropes, as above. (Fig. 1) Pull the ropes and you will see that the smaller of the two ropes will not hold, but slips out, so the thing to do is to give that smaller rope an extra twist, so it will hold.

Take the end of the smaller rope (A) and cross it under the other piece of the same rope at (B), and then up and over the loop of the bigger rope at (C). This will make one end of the small rope on top and one underneath the loop of the bigger rope, and as you pull the knot tight this extra turn will hold that small end in place. *Be sure to make the extra twist with the smaller rope.* (But try it the other way if you want to see what will happen!)   (Fig. 2)

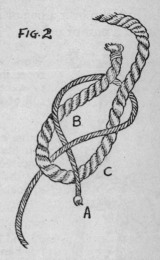

FIG. 2

The name "sheet bend" comes from sailing days—a number of the ropes used to rig a ship are called "sheets" (and you are a landlubber if you call them "ropes"!). "Bending" is a way of making a loop.

There are a number of ways to make a sheet bend; the one shown here is used in joining the ends of two ropes. The "weaver's" knot is a sheet bend tied by weavers using a special method.

BOWLINE

This knot is used when you need a loop in the end of a rope. Its special feature is that it will not pull tight, but will remain the size you make it.

Use it to slip over a peg or hook, or make the loop *around* a post or pole.

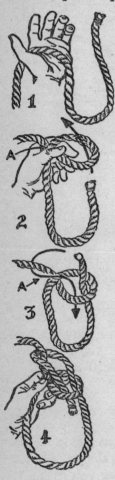

Work with just one end of the rope; the other end may be tied to something else, or may be a coil or long length of rope.

Judge how big a loop you want, and place left hand at about the place you want the knot to come. Let the rope lie across the palm of your left hand.   (Fig. 1)

With the right hand, make a loop up and back of the fingers of the left hand, coming down in front, and catching the rope with the left thumb as it crosses over. (Fig. 2)

Let the fingers slip out of the loop, and take the end of the rope in the right hand, holding at point (A) with left thumb and finger. Pass the end of rope up from underneath into the small loop.   (Fig. 3)

Pull this end to make the main loop of knot the size you will want it, and then pass the end in back of the standing part of rope and back to the front and down into the small loop again so that it lies beside itself.   (Fig. 4)

Take these two pieces of rope in one hand and the main part of rope in the other, and pull in opposite directions to pull knot tight. **(Fig. 5)**

If you want that loop to be around something, as around a bar, pass the end around the bar before you put it through the small loop; pull it as tight as you want it, then proceed as above. **(Fig. 6)**

Sailors learn to make this knot with one hand as they hold on to the rigging with the other. Perhaps you will want to progress to that!

Be sure to learn this knot with just *one* end of the rope; don't use both.

CLOVE HITCH

This is used to make fast an end of rope, as in starting a lashing or tying a rope to a post. Avoid using it when one end is tied to something that moves, like a boat or a horse, as the movement will tend to loosen the knot. A *clove hitch* will stay in place when tight, and will not move up and down the post. Do this knot with *just one end*, too; let the length of rope hang down.

Take one end in right hand, letting rest of rope lie across left palm. Pass end around the back of post from right to left, and back to the front again; cross it over the part in left hand, making an X. (Fig. 1) Hold that X loosely away from the post, with thumb on top, index finger under the X, pointing to the right.

Make another turn around the post, from right to left, this time lower than the first turn, bringing end around and under the X, between the two turns, so that the end points to the right (or in same direction finger pointed), and the long piece of rope leads off left. (Fig. 2)

Pull these ropes in opposite directions. (Fig. 3)

You will want to pull the long end directly from the center of the knot; to do so may require moving knot around the post. To do this, loosen knot by pushing both ends of the rope toward the center of the knot at X. Then swing knot around until it is in desired position. (Fig. 4)

To make a clove hitch on a horizontal bar, follow the same general directions, starting by passing the end over, and in back, of bar. (Fig. 5-6)

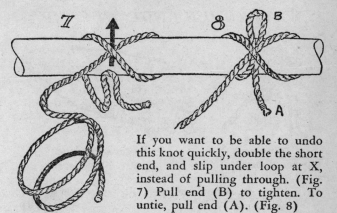

If you want to be able to undo this knot quickly, double the short end, and slip under loop at X, instead of pulling through. (Fig. 7) Pull end (B) to tighten. To untie, pull end (A). (Fig. 8)

You may find some one to show you how to make this knot slip *over* the top of a post—it's easy!

Here are two more—easy to make, and very useful—

Two half hitches
Use to make rope fast to a ring or a post. One half hitch is often used to give extra holding power to a knot.

Overhand knot
Use to keep end from raveling, or as a "stopper" at any place in rope.

WAYS TO USE KNOTS IN CAMP

A permanent
loop for a hook

To tie a bandage

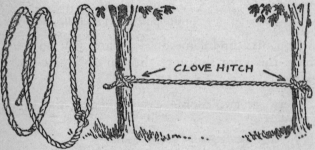

CLOVE HITCH

A loop for the end of a
lifeline

A clothesline

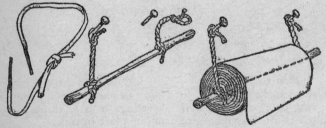

To mend a shoe
lace

A holder for paper

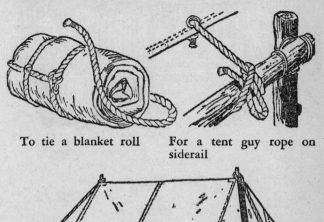

To tie a blanket roll

For a tent guy rope on siderail

Putting up a pup tent

Next steps in knot-tying—

Get a book on knots; learn some other knots. Read a little about the history of knots, and some of the ways they are used.

Learn to *splice a rope*.

Learn the netting knot, or a lanyard knot, and make a craft article.

Learn different types of rope—cotton, hemp, linen, and so forth. Visit a hardware store and ask the salesman to tell you about ropes.

CHAPTER 8

Lashing

WHEN you need a camp table, a coat hanger or a basin rack or some fixin's and furnishin's for your camp site, you'll be glad you know lashing. And it is a sign of a good campcrafter to make something out of the materials you find around you—and to have them fit into the woodland surroundings.

Lashing is a method of fastening sticks or poles together by binding with cord—not with nails, so it is good to use on living trees; easily taken apart, so it is good for a temporary structure; rustic looking, so it fits into camp. A *good* lashing is neat and attractive and holds securely. Campcrafters like it because it can be put together or taken down easily, and requires few tools in the making.

112

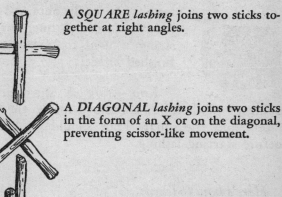

A *SQUARE lashing* joins two sticks together at right angles.

A *DIAGONAL lashing* joins two sticks in the form of an X or on the diagonal, preventing scissor-like movement.

A *SHEER* or *ROUND lashing* joins two sticks along the length of one, rather than at an angle.

A *CONTINUOUS lashing* holds several small sticks at right angles to a long stick.

Materials used depend on the size of the article to be made, on the use to which it will be put, and, to some extent, on what is handy. Strings and twigs will be used in making small craft articles like picture frames, while heavy cord and strong saplings will be used for articles like tables or seats. *Binder twine,* a shaggy kind of cord used in farming, is often used because it is cheap, very tough, and easily obtained in a hardware store. A finer cord or string is used to give a more finished effect.

Knot-tying is the starting point of all lashing; the clove hitch, the half hitch, and the square knot should be learned before starting lashing.

Here's how to learn:

1. Get three sticks about as thick as your thumb, and 12 inches long (the straighter and smoother, the better).

2. Have a piece of cord about 36 inches long.

3. Start with square lashing. Get some one to help you, if you can, or figure it out from the pictures—the other types will be easy.

4. When you have done the lashing once, take it out and try several times before finishing it off.

5. Look it over—get the "feel" of it.

6. Make something simple like a coat hanger or a towel rack.

7. Get your gang to help make something like a camp table.

SQUARE LASHING

Place sticks in position. (Fig. 1)
Tie clove hitch to vertical stick
at one end of cord, slipping knot
around so that the long length of the
cord pulls directly out from the knot.
Be sure you do not pull back *against*
the knot, but pull so that you tighten
the knot. (Fig. 1)

Bind sticks together by passing the
cord down in front of horizontal stick,
under, out to back of upright, around
upright and out to front, (*under* the
horizontal stick) then up, in front of
horizontal stick, in back of upright, and
cord is at starting point. (Fig. 2) Repeat this winding several times, following the first turns, and pulling tightly,
as you make the cord lie neatly beside
previous turns. Be sure to follow the
"square" you have made, and do not
cross the cord over the center of the
sticks, either on the top or underneath.
(Fig. 3 and 4)

When the sticks are firmly bound,
tighten the binding with a *frapping*.
This is done by winding the cord *between* the two sticks, so the first binding is pulled tighter together. (Fig. 5)

End by making two half hitches
around one stick, or by joining the end
of binding cord to the starting end by
a square knot. Clip off, and tuck the
ends underneath the lashing.

DIAGONAL LASHING

Place sticks in position, forming an X, and hold them in this position continually. (Fig. 6)

Make a clove hitch around the two sticks, as shown. (Fig. 6) Make three or four turns around one fork (Fig. 7), then three or four turns around the other fork, pulling tightly. (Fig. 8)

Frap and end as in a square lashing.

SHEER OR ROUND LASHING

Place sticks in desired position.

Start with a clove hitch around one stick. Take several turns around both sticks, making sure the turns lie tightly and neatly beside each other.

Frap, and end with two half hitches or by joining ends with a square knot, tucking both ends under the lashing.

CONTINUOUS LASHING

Have sticks cut and ready, long ones the desired length, short ones the size desired for the width of the finished article, and approximately all the same diameter. Mark or notch the long sticks at even intervals where the small sticks will be lashed to make the small sticks fit into place. (Fig. 2)

Take a cord approximately four times longer than the long stick. (This will vary with the size of the sticks and the cord.)

Start with a clove hitch at one end of the long stick at the *middle of the cord,* so there are equal lengths on either side of the long stick. Place this hitch so that the ends of the cord pull the knot tight as they come up from the under side of the long stick. (Fig. 3)

Bringing the cords around from this knot, pull them over the first small stick, following the lines of the long stick. (Fig. 4). Pull down and under, crossing the cord on the under side of the long stick (Fig. 5) and coming up again, ready to bind the second small stick. Pull cords over the second small stick in the same manner, following the lines of the long stick, going under,

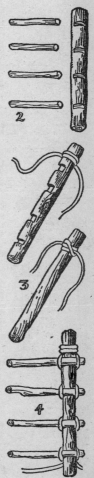

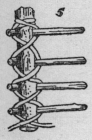

crossing underneath the long stick, and coming up ready for the third stick. Continue this to the end of the small sticks so that the cord always runs parallel to the long stick on the top and crosses on the under side. Pull tightly at each small stick.

End by two half hitches, and tuck ends of cord under last small stick.

A FEW THINGS TO LASH

COAT HANGER
Select two sticks, as illustrated, one with a natural fork, and the other very smooth and slightly curved. Trim ends smoothly. For best results, notch at joining point. Use square lashing.

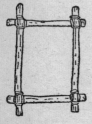

PICTURE OR MIRROR FRAME
Select four smooth twigs or branches. Trim neatly, making them the desired size. Notch at joining points.
Use square lashings, binding with string or fine cord for small frames.

Use same principle for SHOE RACK or SUITCASE RACK.
Suitcase rack, to raise suitcase off damp ground or to prevent scraping on floor.

Shoe rack, to facilitate sweeping floor, keep tent tidy, etc. Raise in back by small pegs.

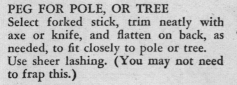

PEG FOR POLE, OR TREE
Select forked stick, trim neatly with axe or knife, and flatten on back, as needed, to fit closely to pole or tree. Use sheer lashing. (You may not need to frap this.)

RACK FOR TOWELS, SWIM SUITS, ETC. or for
keeping lunches, sweaters, etc. off ground on day hikes. Use square lashings. Look for two convenient trees, or make a set of tripods with diagonal lashings.

A TRIPOD BASIN RACK

Select three sturdy sticks, about same thickness. Trim to same length, and smooth off rough spots. Leave forks that may be utilized for hanging up wash cloths, etc. Point at ends if the rack is to be used outdoors.

Hold with hand, and spread apart to judge height wanted. Try a basin on the top, and mark place for lashing which will bring basin to right height.

Lash all three sticks together in a sheer type lashing. Then spread sticks apart evenly in a tripod, and bind as in a diagonal, lashing two ways to hold in place.

Drive points in ground, or strengthen if necessary by braces at the sides (square or diagonal lashing).

Another way to make a tripod is to bind all three sticks together and then twist the middle pole until the lashing is tight. Spread as above. One twist will probably do it.

BRACES FOR TABLES, WOODPILES ETC.

Use diagonal lashings.

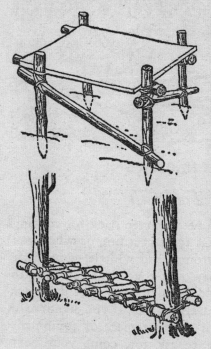

A TABLE TOP FOR THE KITCHEN OR A SEAT Cut and trim all pieces as needed. T w o convenient trees are a big help, or you will need four sturdy posts and possibly braces on side. The two side sticks must be s t r o n g, and as straight as possible. Notch the places for the smaller cross sticks for better results. Lash these in place with square lashing first. Use continuous lashing for top.

Go on from here.

When you know the steps in the four types of lashing, begin to take pride in well-trimmed ends (good use for your sharp jackknife).

Learn what trees grow the best, straightest, smoothest sticks for lashings. Learn what to cut, how to cut, and where—for good conservation.

Be on the lookout for odd shapes of branches, good forks, and so on, to make more interesting articles.

CHAPTER 9

Toolcraft

WHEN you need a green stick for cooking or shavings to start a fire, or when you want to just sit around and whittle, your knife is on call. You may own a jackknife or a sheath knife, and if you do, you'll know that it is your most useful campcrafting tool. If you do not own one, it probably is the first piece of equipment you are planning to ask for, come your next birthday or Christmas. And to do good camp-crafting, you will need one, one you keep for your own use, one you keep in good working condition.

You will use other tools in camping, too, and an axe will come next, either a hand axe or a lightweight long-handled axe to use with both hands. (No two people agree on which is better to start with; you will have to decide for your-self!)

Using any sharp-edged implement means *responsibility*—responsibility for your own safety and that of other people. A campcrafter learns to use tools safely, knows how to take care of them, and knows how to keep them in good working condition. He doesn't need to apologize because his knife won't "cut butter," or because his axe has a large nick in it. A good campcrafter has respect for property, too; he doesn't go slashing around, carving initials or just playing with his knife for something to do. A campcrafter respects living things, and he takes what he needs and no more; he appreciates the beauty of wood, and he leaves it as he finds it on buildings or fences.

Here are things you'll want to know or do about any tool—

1. Know *what* it is for—know each part of it.
2. Know how to oil, clean, sharpen, or whatever is necessary to do to put it in good shape and keep it so.
3. Know how to handle it skillfully.
4. Know precautions about using it safely.
5. Know what to do with it when not in use.
6. Practice—make things with it; practice some more.

There is an old saying that a good craftsman is known by his tools; a good campcrafter is known, too, by the way he handles them and takes care of them.

KNIVES

There are a number of kinds of knives. See how many you and your friends or fellow campers can gather, and look them all over. Most common are jackknives, and sheath or hunting knives. Jackknives fold, so the blade is carried inside the handle; sheath knives are straight, do not fold, and generally have a leather sheath in which they are carried.

SOME TYPES OF KNIVES:

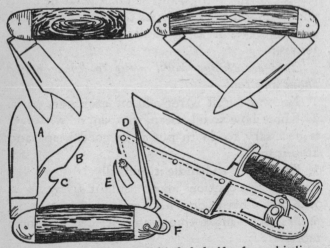

Two-bladed knife; small-bladed knife for whittling; four-bladed knife with (a) blade, (b) screwdriver, (c) bottle opener, (d) awl, (e) can opener, (f) ring for belt; sheath knife (not a jackknife; blade does not fold into handle).

TO CLEAN AND OIL A KNIFE:

DON'T

For a jackknife, put a drop of machine oil on the hinge, and work blade open and shut a few times; it should work easily. For any knife: clean blade with drop of oil and piece of tissue or cloth and steel wool. Don't rub in dirt or sand; this may chip blade.

TO SHARPEN A KNIFE:

Use some kind of a sharpening stone; your mother may let you use her kitchen stone, or you may find another for your own. Sharpening stones are known as hones, oil stones, whetstones or Carborundum. They are made to provide a grinding surface, and come in varying degrees of coarseness. Coarse stones are used for heavy tools, like axes; fine stones for knives or for finishing the edge. Oil or water is sometimes used to reduce the friction, especially for axes. Sometime you'll want a small pocket stone to keep with you all the time, so you can work on your knife or axe any time you are sitting around.

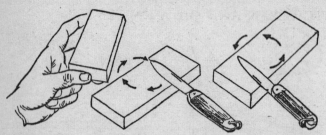

Hold stone with thumb and forefinger *below* the top edge. Hold knife blade flat on stone. Move with circular motion, with pressure away from the knife edge. Turn blade and repeat circular motion on other side.

Keep this up at least three times longer than you think is necessary! To test the edge, try on a piece of wood, not your finger. Try to get a long thin edge that spreads evenly back to the thickest part of blade; the marks of the stone should show all across the blade. (There are many ways to sharpen a knife; get some experienced person to show you his way; then figure out the way you think is best.)

If there is a nick in the blade, use a coarse stone and tip the blade at an angle. Wear away enough of the edge of blade along its length to make an even edge. Finish off with a fine stone.

USING A JACKKNIFE: (Except for opening and closing, the sheath knife is used in the same way.)

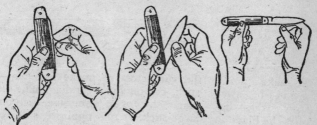

Hold knife in both hands, right thumbnail in slot; pull blade out; keep hold with both hands until open.

TO CLOSE: Reverse above, holding blade until it is nearly closed, then letting it snap shut. Avoid closing with *one* hand. Keep fingers in *back* of edge.

TO USE A KNIFE:

Don't

Take a firm grasp on the handle. Push with your whole hand.

NOT with your thumb. (You don't get the same push.)

Whittle away from you (until you are an expert!). Be sure that nothing (your leg, another camper, a branch) is in the way of the sweep your knife will take if it slips. Move your hand over the arc the knife might cover, just to be sure.

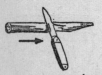

To make a point, whittle away from you, digging the blade in as you go down the stick, and turning stick as you cut, to make an even point.

To cut across a stick, cut on the diagonal. For a large stick, or to

make a notch—cut diagonally on one side, then on opposite side to make a V. Slant cut; don't try to cut straight across.

To make shavings, try to get long, thin pieces, not little scrubby bits. Dig the blade into the wood a bit, and start on a piece of wood without many knots.

To trim a branch, cut away from the thick end toward the top of branch. Start at bottom and trim down the branch.

When cutting a green stick, get it from a thicket, where it will not be missed. Look for one with the kind of fork you will need. Avoid cutting on the edge of a path or a road.

Cut close to the ground, leaving a smooth cut, not a jagged edge.

You may need to make diagonal V-cuts if stick is thick.

WHEN KNIFE IS NOT IN USE:

Usually it is best to close it before laying it down. When you put it aside for a minute, be sure to place it on its *side,* NOT on its back with the blade up (think what might happen!), and NOT stuck in the dirt or sand.

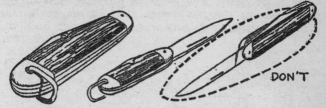

DON'T

TO PASS AN OPEN KNIFE:

The person handing should hold knife by the blade, passing the handle to the other person. In this way the hander has control of the edge of the knife.

The best way to test your knife for sharpness and your hand for skill is to try the knife out on a piece of wood. Start with a piece of kindling wood or a piece of a box end. Make some shavings, or whittle it down to make a round peg. You'll progress to rough sticks from the woods. Can you sharpen a pencil easily, with a good point? That's a good test, too.

When you have made some of the articles shown on pages 140-141, you will want to progress to fancy whittling—balls in boxes, or chain, or woodcarving.

USING A HAND AXE

A HAND AXE is a small axe usually used in one hand. Its flat head can be used as a hammer. It is a handy tool for general use, though for heavy chopping a two-handed axe is necessary. The hand axe presents most of the problems of the two-handed axe *and can be just as dangerous when carelessly used.*

When not in use: DON'T leave it in a tree. DON'T leave it *on* or *in* the ground.

Hang on two nails, or leave in a chopping block, or keep sheathed, or wear on belt, or carry with blade down.

TO SHARPEN A HAND AXE:

Hold axe in left hand by the head; hold sharpening stone in right. Use a rather coarse stone. Work stone on the axe blade. Finish with fine stone. Use a little water on stone to reduce friction.

Hold axe by head. Move stone in circular motion against the edge, keeping it flat on blade. Turn axe, and repeat.

TO USE A HAND AXE:

DON'T

DON'T g r a s p near head of axe!

Grasp end of handle firmly, thumb around fingers. Raise by arm and wrist motion, letting weight of head of axe help to bring it down in place. Sharp, firm blows make for better progress than pecking, ineffectual, quick blows. Take plenty of time. *Be sure to stand and hold axe so that if axe glances or misses, it will not strike your leg or any other part of your body.*

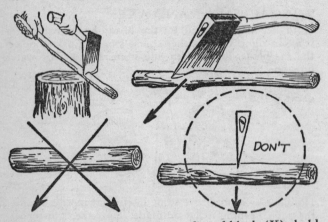

To cut across a stick, strike on edge of block (X); hold at least two feet away from the point you will strike. Make diagonal cuts. Don't try to cut *square across* a stick.

To cut a sapling, clear away brush around it. Make a sharp, diagonal cut down the trunk. Make a second cut up the trunk. Repeat, making cuts larger.

To point a stick, hold at angle on chopping block.
Strike at angle, turning to make a point.

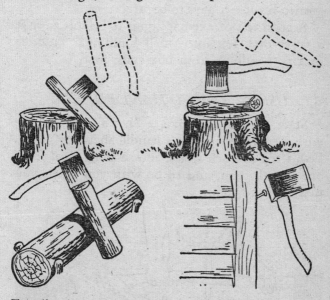

To split a log, place axe on stick; raise both together and
bring down, striking on edge of block. Repeat if necessary. Lay stick flat on block. Do not hold. Raise axe, and
bring down sharply in center of stick. Or lean stick
against a log and strike in center of stick where it touches
the log. The flat part of an axe is a good hammer.

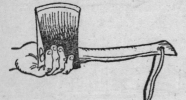

When passing an axe to someone else, the handle goes first.

You may see experts holding a small piece of wood on end to split it; wait until you are an expert to try it—it pays to be safe!

A good test of axemanship is to be able to split a three-inch log into small kindling. Practice making kindling from box ends, first.

USING A TWO-HANDED AXE

Start with a light axe, a "boy's" size, or one with a ½ lb. head and a handle about 24" long. Don't try to learn to use an axe alone—get some one to help you, and to be with you when you first begin to chop.

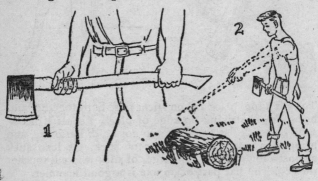

Try first on a small log that is on the ground; put pegs in at four points to keep it steady if it is not heavy enough to stay still.

1. Hold axe easily in both hands, right hand with palm *under* handle at the head, left with palm *over* at end (or reverse if you are left-handed).

2. Stand facing log, feet apart, so weight is even and easy—just far enough away from log to reach it with your arms outstretched and the axe on the log.

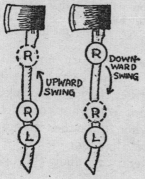

3. Be sure no branches, etc. are overhead or in front or to the side in the arc your axe will swing. Try it to be sure.

4. Practice the swing a few times, just letting the axe fall on log without trying to cut anything—like this:

Count one, two—three, and try to get a good easy, even swing, with no stops between counts.

Count 1—Raise axe head with right hand (at the head) just in front and over your head. Left hand moves up and a little to front—not much. Elbows bent.

Count 2—Let right hand slip down handle to other hand as head of axe falls, with right hand guiding the handle. *Eyes on the spot you want to hit!*

Count 3—As the axe falls (let the weight do the work), straighten elbows (not stiff), and guide axe so it bites into the log.

5. As you get the swing, you will find that you put pressure on at points 2-3 to hit harder. The end of the axe (left hand) will not move very much—the head does the swinging.

Safety Note: Your feet are apart, and your weight distributed evenly so that the axe will slip *between* your legs if it misses the log. Your eyes must be *always* on the spot you want to hit. If you look at your foot when the axe is coming down, you are likely to *hit* that foot.

You'll be good when you can chop through

a five-inch log—easily, and without too many strokes! But it takes a good axe, patience, and plenty of practice. Don't do it alone!

When you're good at this, get some one to help you cut down a small tree. (Practice good conservation in choosing the tree!)

OTHER TOOLS

Here are some other tools you will be using in campcrafting:

FOR MAKING WOOD ARTICLES:

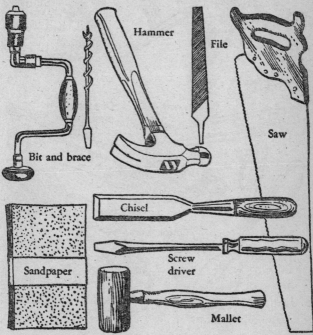

Hammer

File

Bit and brace

Saw

Chisel

Sandpaper

Screw driver

Mallet

FOR WOODPILES:

Sawbuck

Bucksaw

Chopping block

FOR TIN WORK:

Can openers

One that takes
top off clean

Punch type

Cotton work
gloves

Tin shears

FOR SHARPENING TOOLS:

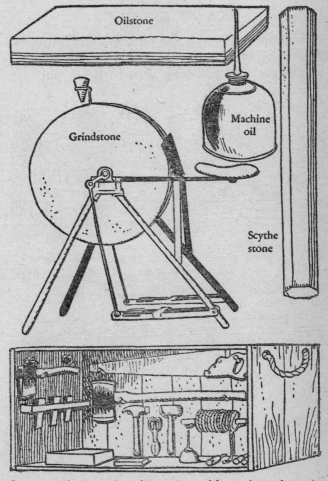

In camp—have a place for tools, and keep them there.

THINGS TO MAKE WITH
KNIFE OR AXE

Use natural woods for pins, buckles, buttons, letter openers. Carve with knife; finish with fine sandpaper and polishing wax to bring out the grain of the wood.

Pins of plain polished wood, carved initial, favorite leaves

Dig out back; put in small safety pin with plastic wood. Smooth off and let harden.

Belt buckles   Napkin ring   Buttons of wood or nuts

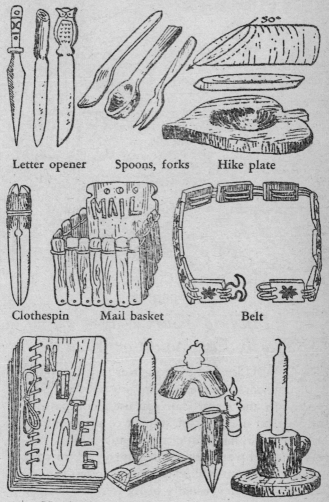

Letter opener   Spoons, forks   Hike plate

Clothespin   Mail basket   Belt

Notebook covers   Candlesticks

CHAPTER 10

Finding Your Way—
North, East, South or West

DO YOU know how to get around? Around outdoors, we mean. Can you tell directions by the sun and stars? Can you use a compass? A campcrafter uses the sun, stars or compass as tools to help him in his campcrafting and hiking. Perhaps you will want the rising sun to peek in your tent. Perhaps you will want to place your tent so the east winds that usually bring rain are not going to enter the front. If you have been hiking west all morning, it may be helpful to know how to go back east to reach home. If your road directions say "turn north at the end of road," you may wish you knew in *which* direction north lies.

ANYWHERE, ANYTIME—if you *do* know north, you can find the other directions e a s i l y. Face NORTH, and EAST is at your *right;* WEST is at your *left;* SOUTH is in back of you.

Now to find the directions—

BY THE SUN

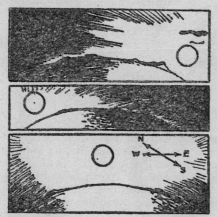

(This gives you general directions, not specific or accurate ones.) In the morning the sun is in the EAST; in the afternoon, in the WEST; and at noon, overhead, slightly toward the south.

If you stand with your right shoulder toward the sun in the morning, or with your left shoulder toward the sun in the afternoon, you will be facing NORTH, and SOUTH is in back of you. Your shadow will fall east or west, in the opposite direction.

BY YOUR WATCH

(This is more accurate.)
1. Hold watch level in the sun.
2. Hold a twig or blade of grass over the center point of the watch, so a shadow falls on face.
3. Slowly turn the watch until the shadow lies over the HOUR HAND. North is the point halfway between the hour hand, as it then points, and the twelve on the face of the watch (going around the watch the shortest way—one way in the morning, the other way in the afternoon).

BY THE STARS

At night the North Star will tell you where north is. Get some one to help you find the constellation known as the Big Dipper. The two "pointers" of this dipper always point to the Pole Star, or North Star. Face it, and you can find the other directions. Seafaring men used this star to steer their ships in olden days.

BY A COMPASS

A compass is a watch-like instrument which has a magnetized needle that always points to the north. (Ask your science teacher to explain why.) There are many kinds of compasses—the very intricate and accurate

mariners' or engineers' compasses, and the very simple kind that you can get at many stores. Many compasses have a stationary printed face, something like a watch. The points of the compass are printed on the face. A needle with an arrow or point on one end swings around a peg in the center. Some have a dial on which the needle is fastened, and the whole compass face swings around.

To use a compass with a needle:

1. Face the object or direction you want to know about.

2. Hold compass in front of you, *level,* so needle swings freely.

3. The needle will swing back and forth, and finally come to a stop. IT THEN POINTS NORTH (even though you don't turn around!).

4. Now turn the compass carefully (keeping needle in same position) until the N (or sometimes a spearhead) printed on the face of the compass is UNDER THE NEEDLE. This is called "orienting or setting the compass," and makes the compass face point in the right directions.

The compass face generally has a mark that shows north clearly; if it does not, figure out by the sun where north is, and you can tell how your own compass is marked.

5. Keep compass in this "oriented" or "set" position, and point a twig or pencil from edge of compass toward the direction of object. The end of the twig at the compass edge will point to the

direction of the object or path. This is called "sighting with a compass."
(If the needle and dial swing together, you will skip step 4.)

Take care of your compass—it is a delicate instrument, and should be handled with care if you hope to keep it accurate. If it has a way of locking the needle, so it does not swing freely when not in use, be sure to use it. Many compasses have cases that close, like a watch; this case protects the glass, and is good to have.

Try to see a mariner's compass, and see how the compass is suspended in the box, so it will always be level, no matter how the ship rolls.

"Boxing a compass" means being able to recite all the directions in good order. Learn to do it.

Reading and making maps may be good skills for you to learn next. Learn to use topographical maps. Trailing and cross-country hiking make use of direction-finding, too, and will be good fun. "Orienteering" is a sport that combines all of these skills; it is very popular in Sweden where it started, and is growing in popularity in this country.

CHAPTER 11

Camping Places and Equipment

SOME DAY, we hope, you will have a chance to go camping—with your family, with your scout troop if you belong to one, with your club, or to a summer camp, for several weeks or the whole summer. You may have the fun of developing a campsite with some other campers; you may go on trips where you will make or use temporary shelters and cooking places; you may sleep in tents or cabins that are all ready for you when you arrive. Wherever and however you camp, good "campkeeping" and good care of your equipment are signs of good campcrafting.

AN OUTDOOR KITCHEN

Perhaps your first camping place will be in your yard, or some other spot near home, where the first thing you'll make will be an outdoor or trail stove and kitchen. At a summer camp your tent, unit or small group may develop such a kitchen near your living quarters, so it will be fun and easy to cook out as often as you want to plan it. Wherever your outdoor kitchen, you'll want these things in it:

A stove

A woodpile

Storage places for equipment and for food if you keep staple things like sugar, salt and so on, there.

A table or work space.

A drain for dishwater and other liquids.

Those are the first things; you may want to add a cupboard, a "cup-tree," a "pan-tree," another fireplace, such as one for baking, etc.

KITCHEN "FURNISHINGS"

Here are some ideas—

A cupboard for dishes, kettles, salt, sugar and the like
may be made of packing boxes or built to order. Here
is a good portable one. The front lets down to make
a work table. Cover the top with water-proof material.

A cup-tree   A pan-tree

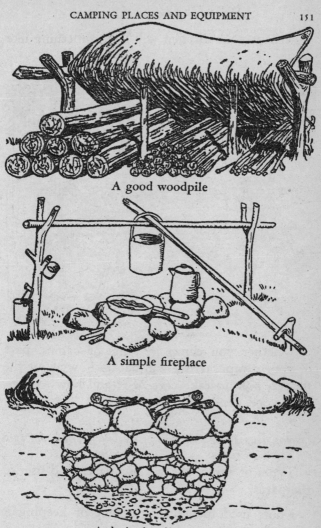

A good woodpile

A simple fireplace

A drain for dishwater

Perhaps your kitchen will look something like this:

Whether you camp in tents or cabins, part of your campcrafting will be to know about the shelter, how to take care of it and how to keep it in good condition.

If you live in tents, you may learn these things:

Types of tents, the various parts, and uses of the parts.

Knots used in erecting a tent or keeping it trim.

How to roll and tie flaps or tent walls.

How to take care of canvas, wet or dry, and something about canvas or duck.

How to pitch a tent, peg it down, ditch it; how to make it look "trim."

How to put up mosquito tents or netting.

Here are some helps for wall tents, which are the usual kind found in established camps; learn about your own type of tent.

Some good things to know about CANVAS:

Pins in canvas make holes for the rain to come through and may start tears.

Running the finger or foot down the roof of the tent when it is wet will break the air bubbles that make the canvas waterproof, and there will be a leak.

Canvas mildews when rolled up damp. After a rain, let the sides and flaps dry before rolling them again.

Field mice like to live in tents, too! Watch your tent flaps in a long spell of pleasant weather; unroll them, and let them air once in a while.

Canvas and ropes shrink when wet, so ropes should be loosened at the beginning of a storm, and tightened again afterwards. Pull ropes evenly on both sides to keep the tent looking trim.

The tent should fit loosely when dry, so the sides may be pegged down to floor or floor pegs easily.

Nails tend to split tent poles—use lashings. Remove lashings or nails before folding tents away.

When folding tents, be sure the canvas is dry. Let sun shine on the canvas for two hours after dew has disappeared. Fold on seams smoothly. Brush cobwebs, insects, dirt, etc. off canvas before folding.

If you live in a cabin at camp, you may learn these things:
How to care for whatever equipment is there —screens, curtains, shutters, etc. in sunny, wet or windy weather; how to roll and tie canvas screens; or how to fasten shutters.

How to put up shelves in a good craftsmanlike manner, making pegs instead of using nails.

Making drains to prevent water from dripping from roofs.

How to put up mosquito tents.

How to make shoe racks, suitcase racks, etc.

In log cabins, how to keep the chinking in good repair.

CAMPING SHELTERS

You may make a camp in your yard. Your family may have a tent, and all of you may go off for a fine camping holiday; you may go to an established camp, or your troop or group may have equipment for camping. There are many kinds of camping shelters, from the pup tent put up for just a night or two to big wall tents put up for the summer at a camp; cabins and other wooden structures are also used.

Here are some temporary hike shelters you may be using:

A Poncho Shelter   An Explorer's Tent

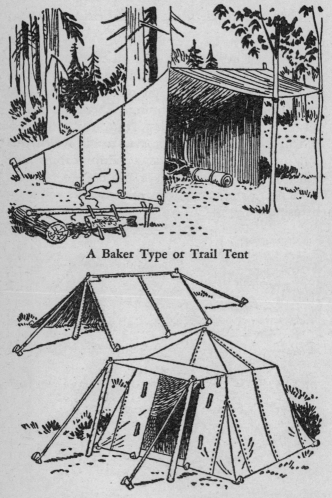

A Baker Type or Trail Tent

"Pup" Tent   An Umbrella Tent

Here are some other more permanent types of camp shelters:

An Indian Tepee   Wall Tent

Adirondack Lean-to

Conical Tent
(Erected with a center pole)

WALL TENTS

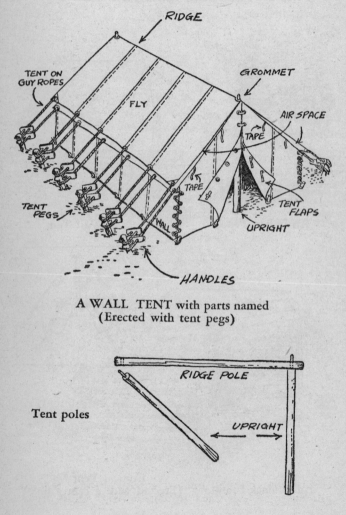

RIDGE

TENT ON GUY ROPES

GROMMET

FLY

AIR SPACE

TAPE

TAPE

TENT PEGS

WALL

UPRIGHT

TENT FLAPS

HANDLES

A WALL TENT with parts named
(Erected with tent pegs)

Tent poles

RIDGE POLE

UPRIGHT

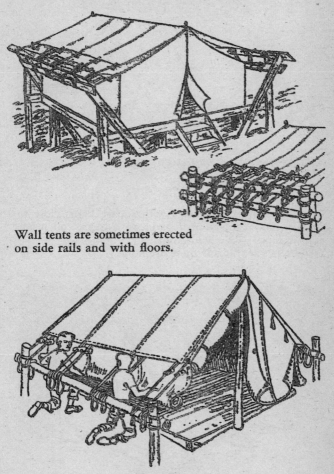

Wall tents are sometimes erected
on side rails and with floors.

To roll tent:

Unlace corner ropes; unhook ropes fastening tent to
ground pegs. Roll sides, rolling the edge inside, away

from the rollers. Tie tapes with square knots close to roof of tent. Fold front flaps in on corners; roll inside and tie tapes with square knots.
(Add tapes at seams if there are none.)

Ditch tents without floors, to keep rain from running across inside ground.

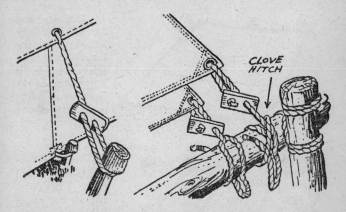

CLOVE HITCH

Tents are erected by pegs or on siderails. The wooden handle is to tighten or loosen ropes.

HOW TO PITCH A WALL TENT:

1. Choose the right place. With a piece of cord make an outline of the floor size of the tent; for a 9 x 12 tent, put a loop in the cord at 12 ft., another at the next 9 ft.,

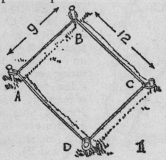

another at 12 ft., and join with beginning at next 9 ft. Four campers take cord by the loops (A-B-C-D) and stretch it over ground. Turn as needed, to find best place for tent. (9 ft. ends will be the front and back). Put pegs in ground to show the four corners of tent floor (A-B-C-D).

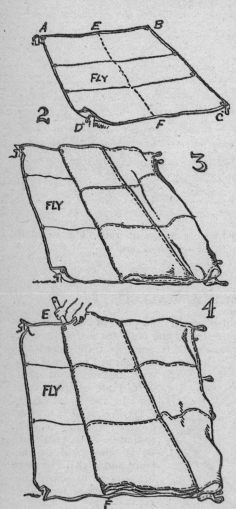

2. Unfold and spread FLY upside-down on the spot, so the RIDGE E-F is approximately over the A-B line or a little above it.

3. Unfold and place TENT on fly, so the ridge of tent lies over the ridge of fly. Tent should lie on one side, not opened up like the fly.

4. Push RIDGE POLES carefully through tent (below the stitching of seams if there is no opening) and fitting corners of ridge pole into corners of tent, eyes of pole at grommets of tent (metal rings at E and F).

5. Place UP-RIGHTS in both ends, pins through the eyes of the ridge pole, and through the grommets of the tent at E and F.

6. Swing edge (G-H) of fly down on top of tent, and put pins of poles through grommets of fly (E and F).

7. Ends of up-rights should be at center of front and back of tent floor. Move whole tent with poles so that they are at points I-J.

(Be sure there are no wrinkles or pleats in tent or fly on the ridge pole.)

8. With two campers at each pole (one places foot at end of pole, one with hands higher up) raise tent so it is erect, ends of uprights at I and J.

9. One (or two) campers hold tent poles steady, and two (or four) pull corner ropes of tent out at angle.

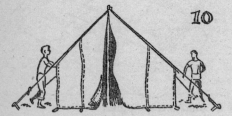

10. Like this— put four tent pegs in temporarily at an angle, and attach loops of corner ropes.

11

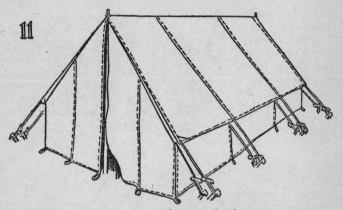

11. "Square up" the tent, to be sure the four corner ropes are spaced evenly, and when pulled tight, make the tent trim and square.

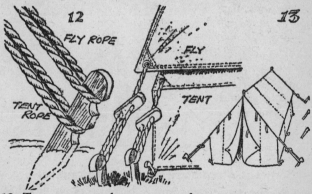

12. Tent pegs may have two notches; tent ropes go on lower notches, fly ropes on upper ones. Or you may use two rows of single pegs, one for tent, one for fly.

13. Put pegs for side ropes in a line between corner pegs, so the ropes pull at right angles to tent or fly.

14. Use wooden handles to pull ropes evenly. Have some one go out in front, and check to be sure tent is trim, ropes pulled evenly on all sides.

15. Put pegs in ground at tent floor directly under loops in hem of tent. Put loops in place when tent is not rolled up.

16. Tent poles should be at right angles to ground —if they lean, the ropes are pulled too hard on one side.

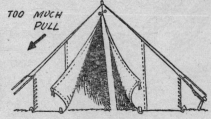

TOO MUCH PULL

Sometimes tents are put up with railings—

Use the same procedure, but use clove hitches to tie to railings. Some camps reverse the ropes, so wooden handles are near tent. Trim the ends of ropes, or wrap neatly, to give shipshape look to tent. (See page 101.)

Tent with railing for ropes.

Tent on tent platform.   Loops at hem go on nails
or pegs.

When tent has a fly, there should be an air space between tent and fly to give added protection from rain and to keep roof of tent cooler.

There are many different ideas on how to place tent pegs. Talk with counselors or some other informed people to find out how your group does it.

MAKE YOUR CAMP COMFORTABLE!

Shelf for a tent, for sweaters, bathrobes, etc.

A clothes drier made from a small dead cedar tree.

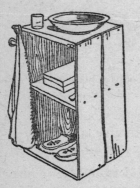

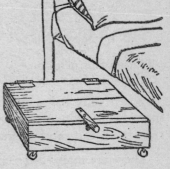

A "bureau" from an orange crate. You may not want a curtain in snake country.

A box on casters for under the bed.

A shoe bag holds all odd bits of equipment in handy fashion.

A good camper covers his pillow and sheets with a dark blanket to keep them dry and clean.

Mosquito Netting Frames.

(See also *Lashings* on page 112)

OTHER "FURNISHINGS"

Seats and stools for tent or campfire circle.

A wastebasket
of lashed twigs.

A broom
made of twigs.

A sundial on
a log.

Letters for signs of twigs or blocks of wood.

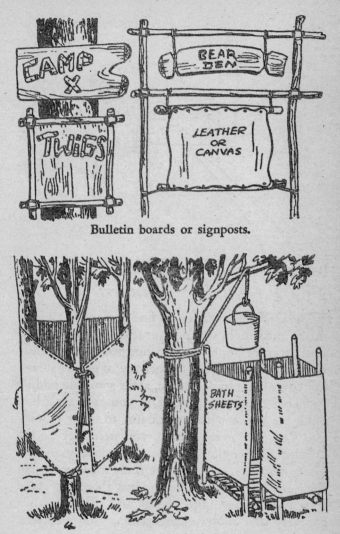

Bulletin boards or signposts.

Showers or bath shelters.

CHAPTER 12

Outdoor Manners

DID YOU ever try to find a place for a picnic lunch, stopping at several spots only to find litters of papers and orange peels and bottles? Did you ever watch a farmer try to get his straying cows back in a pasture, after someone hadn't bothered to close a gate? Did you ever see a boy poking a snake with a stick just to make it wiggle? Did you ever——but you need not be reminded of people with poor outdoor manners. There are those who forget their manners when they get out into the open, and there are those who treat people and things and places with a courtesy that shows appreciation. Campcrafters, of course, are familiar with good outdoor behavior and manners.

There is more to outdoor behavior than just good manners; there is the angle of good sensible safety and care, and of not taking chances that will make it difficult for you or for other people. Call it manners or behavior, or citizenship—it all adds up to the way you act when you are out. Good campcrafters have a code for such behavior; like all good manners, the code begins with thinking of others and acting as you would like others to act toward YOU or your property.

GETTING ABOUT

When you walk by yourself, you have little difficulty getting along without disturbing someone else. When you go hiking or walking with a group, you present another picture; you present greater difficulties to car drivers or to pedestrians. So it is well to know some rules of the road that will help you all get where you want to go, and to get there by the simplest, safest way. Here are some hints:

On sidewalks, break up into twos and threes, and don't spread across so that people coming in the opposite direction can't get by.

At crosswalks, wait together for a light to change, or for a chance to cross. Don't straggle across.

Along a highway walk on the left, facing traffic, in twos or threes, dropping behind each other in a single line if oncoming traffic needs to come close.

At night, wear something white like an armband, or carry a flashlight.

When with leaders, have one at the front and one at the end of the line. Put those with the shortest legs in front. Or let the long-legged hikers go on ahead in one group.

Don't thumb rides.

On buses and trains keep together, and remember that the other people in the bus may not wish to be "entertained" by your songs, cheers and screams. When your private bus goes through city streets, you are in the public eye. Save your singing until you are out on the open road.

When riding bicycles, know and obey traffic regulations.

OUT IN THE COUNTRY

Leave things as you find them—or leave them improved.

Be sure to leave gates closed or open, as you find them. This is VERY important to the farmer.

Get permission to go on private property.

Stick to paths when going across farm land, especially fields of hay or grain; go around the edges of fields when there is no path.

Apples on trees, cucumbers on vines, flowers in yards are all private property! Some people think anything that grows is public property.

Except when you know how to go across country, keep to trails in the woods. Leave trail signs and markers as you find them, unless you help put them in better condition for other hikers.

Check back to the notes on fire building and fire safety, and be sure you know how to put them into practice.

Leave trunks of trees and wooden walls and fences without the benefit of your initials or other whittlings.

Don't strip bark from living trees.

Leave your picnic site or campsite as you wish you had found it—clean, no rubbish, no garbage, supply of fuel for the next fellow.

Live and let live—don't kill or harm or bother or needlessly destroy things and creatures that grow in the open.

Help make your yard or your camp a wildlife sanctuary, where birds and animals find shelter and food—and friends.

SAFETY OUTDOORS

Watch out for water—carry it with you in a canteen, or get it from a public supply, or make it pure with some purifying agent such as Clorox. Don't drink from just any well or brook. Two drops of Clorox to a gallon of water or special tablets, such as Halazone tablets, will make water safe.

Be careful about the milk you buy—get it pasteurized, to be SURE of it.

If you are in unfamiliar territory, plan to get back to your camp or home well before dark.

If you are lost—don't get panicky; try to think out where you have come from, by the sun or a compass, and go back in the opposite direction. Go down hill rather than up. Following a brook will generally lead to some home or farm or village.

When with a group—have buddies, and do not go so far from the main group that you cannot hear shouts or a whistle. Have prearranged signals—and stick by them.

If one person is hurt, and another goes for help, leave the hurt person as warm and comfortable as possible. Mark the trail well on the way back to camp or the group.

For skiing, canoeing, bicycling and other means of travel, learn first aid, accident prevention, repairs to equipment, etc. before starting out on the trip.

It will all add up to good manners again—don't take chances that may mean that many people will have to risk their lives to help you, because you didn't pay attention, or didn't stick with the others, or tried to be "smart."

Good campcrafters—good outdoor friends!

CHAPTER 13

Our Pioneer Heritage

THERE ARE some of us today whose grand-
mothers can tell true stories of the days when
they were little girls, traveling west with their
families in covered wagons; there are grand-
fathers who can tell of helping to homestead in
some territory; there are members of Indian
tribes who can tell of tribal life on the great
plains. All of them were the campers of other
days. They left us a heritage of living out of
doors, of adventure, of sound bodies and resource-

ful hands and heads. We can catch the spirit and learn much from books and stories that tell of their way of life, their struggles, and their accomplishments. We can follow the great scouts like Kit Carson and Davy Crockett, we can go afield with Sacagawea, we can travel the Oregon Trail in a covered wagon, we can live again with the Pilgrims in the log huts of the early settlements on this continent. You will be especially interested in the books that tell of the settling of your particular part of the country; there are many series such as the "Rivers of America" that tell the tales of the people who ventured forth to find new homes in new territories.

There was adventure a-plenty in the lives of those early settlers; there was good practical outdoor living, too. They cooked over improvised fireplaces; they made their own utensils of wood or shells or clay or gourds; they learned to use tools to make their living easier; they learned what is found for food in the woods and streams; they grew their own food—they lived by their wits, their strength, their resourcefulness. From both their adventure and their practical living the camper of today gains much to make his camping good.

There are so many books that help you catch that pioneering spirit, that tell of early settlers, it is difficult to pick out even a few. But for your armchair reading or to slip in your knapsack for some quiet moment at camp, here are some suggestions:

Abe Lincoln Grows Up by Carl Sandburg (Harcourt, Brace & Co.)

Wagon Train West by Rhoda Louise Nelson (Thomas Y. Crowell)

Schoolhouse in the Woods by Rebecca Candell (John C. Winston)

Mighty Mountain by Archie Binns (Charles Scribner's Sons)

The Land of the Free Series—including *Song of the Pines, Tidewater Valley, I Heard a River,* and *Sign of the Golden Fish* (John C. Winston Co.)

There are books of the crafts and games of early days, too. These suggest many activities for camp, school or club. Here are a few:

Children of the Handcrafts and *Tops and Whistles* by Carolyn Sherwin Bailey (Viking Press)

When Antiques Were Young and *Candle Days* by Marion Nicholl Rawson (E. P. Dutton)

Poems and songs, too, lend their share to our heritage from our pioneering forefathers; here are some collections:

The Fireside Book of Folk Songs by Boni and Lloyd (Simon & Schuster)

My American Heritage by Ralph Henry and Lucile Pannell (Rand McNally)

A Book of Americans by Rosemary and Stephen Benét (Farrar and Rinehart)

I Hear America Singing by Ruth Barnes (John C. Winston)

A Treasury of Folk Songs by Sylvia and John Kolb (Bantam Books)

Another part of our heritage are the dances that have been handed down through the years, and that now are again so much a part of this country's enjoyment, in town and in camp. Square and round dances were holiday and evening fun for early settlers and pioneers. Today we have records that give the music and the calls; we have many groups that meet regularly to enjoy the dances with callers and fiddlers. You can pick them up easily by yourself, too. Ask your physical education teacher to suggest some good books or records. Here are some recommended books:

Dances of Our Pioneers by Grace L. Ryan (A. S. Barnes)

American Country-Dances by Elizabeth Burchenal (G. Schirmer)

Cowboy Dances by Lloyd Shaw (Caxton Printers)

The Country Dance Book by Beth Tolman and Ralph Page (A. S. Barnes)

CHAPTER 14

All Outdoors

LAKES, hills, forests, plains, streams or deserts —all these may be the starting place for your hiking and camping—the whole outdoors. Whatever you do, wherever you go, Mother Nature has many treasures in store for you, if you are interested, if you are curious, if you have imagination. There is no part of camping that is not linked with nature; campcrafters learn to know what is around them, and how it can serve them for usefulness and for happiness. Wonderful new trails are open to you when you begin to STOP, LOOK, and LISTEN to the world around you.

Everything you handle, everything you use, in camp or otherwise, comes from nature—the pencil with which you write, the paper this book is printed on, the chair on which you are sitting, and the food you had for lunch. As you become aware of the out-of-doors, you begin to learn how dependent one thing is upon other things; you begin to realize what remarkable resources are found in nature. And then you find yourself learning something about a very important problem—conservation. There is much talk now about the need for conserving our natural resources in this country, and in the world. This is not idle talk, but it grows from a realization that carelessness and wastefulness have destroyed so much of our forests and lands and streams and wildlife that there is much to be concerned about. You may not think that you can do much about preventing a flood or erosion of land, or about stopping a big forest fire. But there ARE things that you can do, in your own small way, for a good camper is a conservationist. He is frugal with what is plentiful, taking just what he needs, and he protects what is rare, leaving it or helping it to grow. A campcrafter does not needlessly kill anything—an insect on the path or a deer in the woods. He does not slash trees and pull up flowers. He knows that each living thing has a place, and each helps to keep the balance of all things that grow.

When you are a good campcrafter, you are a good conservationist, too. With many other citizens of this country, you may want to take the Conservation Pledge.

Conservation Pledge

I GIVE MY
PLEDGE AS AN AMERICAN
TO SAVE AND FAITHFULLY TO
DEFEND FROM WASTE THE
NATURAL RESOURCES OF
MY COUNTRY – ITS SOIL
AND MINERALS. ITS
FORESTS. WATERS.
AND WILDLIFE

This pledge won first place in a contest held by the OUTDOOR LIFE magazine several years ago. It is now widely accepted and used by organizations interested in conservation. If you would like more information on this, you can get it by writing to *Outdoor Life,* 353 Fourth Ave., New York, N. Y.

When you cut a sapling, consider how you can help other trees to grow by your cutting; when you make a path up a hill, make it a zigzag path rather than straight up and down, so you will keep rains from washing away the soil; when you build fires outdoors, be extra careful so YOU are never guilty of starting a forest fire; —these are ways you can help America keep her natural resources to serve your grandchildren and their grandchildren.

Nature has many uses in campcrafting; it also leads the way to many hobbies or life professions. The scientists of today were the boys and girls of yesterday who liked learning about flowers or stones or insects or birds. There are many, many adults today who find great joy in some hobby that is based on birdlore or rock-finding or wild flowers. A campcrafter's enjoyment of the out-of-doors is based on a general appreciation of the whole outdoors, of the beauty of the countryside, of the interesting things that are in the out-of-doors.

Don't feel that you must be an expert to enjoy nature! You can begin by just looking around you at what is growing, what is on the land, what is in the sky, what is in the water. Soon you will begin to see the same things over again, and you will find that you know a few names. There are books to help in every step—very simple ones that help you begin to know, and more technical ones to help when you have progressed along the nature trail.

Start by getting acquainted. If you see someone you never knew before, or if a friend says, "Say, you'd like to meet so-and-so," you answer: "What's his name? Where is he from? What's he like?" The same thing is true in meeting a bird or a flower or a tree—find out these same three things, name—where it lives—what it is like. Soon you will feel you have met an old friend when that bird flashes by, or you pass that tree, or you find that flower again.

Try to find someone who is already interested in nature to share his enthusiasm with you; if you are in camp, there will be counselors who are interested; if you are in a club or troop, your leader may be able to find someone to come to talk with you; there is undoubtedly someone in your own block who has a garden, knows about snails or toads, or is a stargazer.

DON'T TRY EVERYTHING AT ONCE! Start in by looking, admiring, protecting things in general, and soon you will discover what phase of nature lore you like best. But don't expect to "finish off" something in short order. Some men spend their lives learning about one small part of one of nature's classifications and still feel they have much more to learn. Most of us do not go that far—we just like certain things, and learn something more about them. It isn't so much learning names and other information as it is learning to enjoy and appreciate nature.

One wonderful thing about nature is that it is all around everywhere—all year through, in the city or the country; another is that it is FREE! There is no price of admission to watch a mother bird feeding her babies, to watch the clouds overhead, to lie on pine needles and look up through the branches, or to cool your feet in a brook and watch the water striders busily at work.

There are all sorts of things for you to do to help you learn about nature; this one short chapter can only point out some trail markers to you; you must find people and books to help you—but to start off, here are some ideas:

The campcrafter's tests on page 30 include some nature tests, too. You will notice they are mostly observation, or keeping a record. That is to help you begin to look around—to stop and listen.

Get acquainted with your "neighbors"—the things that grow near your home, your tent, or the hill where you picnic. Learn about your own particular part of the country; nature varies in every section.

Learn to know any poisonous plants or animals in your locality. Learn what they do, how they do it, and you will learn then how to avoid difficulties with them. Most of them are not as bad as they seem when you know how to deal with them, how to avoid them.

Some people like to make lists, collect pictures, make notebooks or diaries. Others prefer gardens or bird feeding stations, or similar activities.

There are many stories and poems about the out-of-doors, and about things that live there.

Wood is a great campcrafting material—you'll want to learn about it, learn to use it well, learn to know why some is hard, why some straight, why some burns well.

Stones, too, will serve you—you'll use them for fireplaces and may discover that some blow up or are not very useful. You'll want to know why.

Weather is always with us—you'll find many interesting activities in forecasting the weather.

If you have a camera, you'll find all sorts of new trails to follow in "shooting" the out-of-doors.

There are things to make—birdhouses and gourd dishes, and things to sketch or paint.

Whether you like birds, beasts or fowl; whether you take an interest in the vegetable, animal or mineral kingdom; whether you make bird and flower lists; or whether you take your enjoyment of nature by observation—you will always be grateful for all of nature, and all of the out-of-doors that makes camping possible.

And, we hope, you will be a good outdoor citizen, as well.

If you are interested in getting good information and help, and if you would like to do a small share toward the big job of protecting wildlife in this country, get in touch with either of these organizations to find out about club or individual memberships:

The National Audubon Society, 1000 Fifth Avenue, New York, N. Y.

Defenders of the Furbearers, 1412 16th Street, NW, Washington 6, D.C.

Books You'll Enjoy

There are so many books on nature and conservation that it is difficult to recommend just a few. Ask in your public or school library for any general nature books or specialized ones they have.

There are many inexpensive books that you may buy to build your own nature library; some are small and easily slipped in your knapsack or pocket. A number of the publishers of 25-cent books are now reprinting nature guides. Sometimes the "dime" stores carry such books, too. Get in the habit of looking at book racks and counters for nature books.

Here are some suggestions for books to get from your library, or for your own library:

GENERAL

The Book of Nature Hobbies by Ted Pettit (Didier).

In Woods and Fields by Margaret Waring Buck (Abingdon-Cokesbury Press).

You will also want to get acquainted with the "Field Books" published by G. P. Putnam; nearly every library has this set.

There are other series of nature books, too, such as the Row, Peterson & Co. series; look for them in your school library.

For general information, turn to the Boy Scout Handbook, the Girl Scout Handbook, or the Book of the Camp Fire Girls; all three have good lists of nature books to help with specific subjects.

SPECIAL

TREES: *Field Book of American Trees and Shrubs* by F. Schuyler Mathews (G. P. Putnam). *Complete Guide to North American Trees* by Carlton Clarence Curtis. New Home Library (Doubleday & Co.).

INSECTS: *Field Book of Insects* by Frank E. Lutz (G. P. Putnam). *The First Book of Bugs* by Margaret Williamson (Franklin Watts). *Ants, Bees, and Wasps* by John Lubbock (E. P. Dutton).

WATER LIFE: *The Field Book of Ponds and*

Streams by Ann Morgan (G. P. Putnam). *Turtles* by Wilfred Bronson (Harcourt Brace and Co.).

BIRDS: *A Guide to the Most Familiar American Birds* by Zim and Gabrielson (Simon & Schuster) —pocket-sized edition, with a special feature of maps showing the areas where birds are found. *Field Guide to the Birds* and *Field Guide to Western Birds* by Roger Tory Peterson (Houghton Mifflin Co.). There is also a pocket-sized edition of the first, *How to Know the Birds* (Mentor).

ANIMALS: *Animal Sounds, Animal Weapons, Animal Tracks*—all by George Mason (William Morrow). *Tracks and Trailcraft* by Ellsworth Jaeger (Macmillan). *Field Book of North American Mammals* by H. E. Anthony (G. P. Putnam).

SNAKES: *Snakes* by Herbert S. Zim (William Morrow). *Snakes Alive and How They Live* by Clifford Pope (Viking Press).

FLOWERS: *Flowers: A Guide to Familiar American Wildflowers* by Zim and Martin (Simon & Schuster). *Field Book of American Wildflowers* by F. Schuyler Mathews (G. P. Putnam).

ROCKS: *Field Book of Common Rocks and Minerals* by Frederic Loomis (G. P. Putnam). *Earth's Adventures* by Carroll Lane Fenton (John Day).

STARS: *A Dipper Full of Stars* by Lou Williams (Wilcox & Follett).

SEASHORE LIFE: *Beginner's Guide to Seashore Life* by Leon Hausman (G. P. Putnam).

There are also a number of nature magazines. *Canadian Nature* is a fine magazine for enthusiastic beginners; it has an edition in the United States called *Outdoors Illustrated* (Published by the National Audubon Society). *Natural History Magazine, Junior Natural History Magazine, Nature Magazine, American Forests* and the *Audubon Magazine* are good ones to look up in the library.

State and Federal conservation, park and forest services have numerous pamphlets which are generally free or cost only a few cents. Write to your own state bureau of information, or to the Superintendent of Documents, Washington 25, D.C., to find out what is available.

CAMPING MANUALS FOR YOU

There are many camping books that will be good additions to your own library. They will help you go beyond the first steps shown in this book. As you advance along the camping trail, you will want to know more of camping. Here are books to own or to borrow:

The manuals of the national youth organizations, the Boy Scouts of America, the Camp Fire Girls, the Girl Scouts of the U.S.A., the Youth

Hostel Association. Look especially for the *Scout Field Book* of the Boy Scouts, *The Outdoor Book* of the Camp Fire Girls, and *Cooking Out of Doors* of the Girl Scouts.

Other sources of information:

CAMPCRAFT ABC'S—for Camp Counselors (published by Girl Scouts of USA), by Catherine T. Hammett, is a manual from which much of this book has been adapted.

Organizations of hiking and camping groups in your locality. Look up their material when you find out about their membership and activities.

Services such as state and federal forestry and park departments. Write to your State House for help on your state's publications, and to the U.S. Forest Service, Washington, D.C., for a list of publications and other material that is available.

Companies that sell camping equipment, such as knives, rope, tents, sleeping bags, etc., often have pamphlets that are free. Food companies have special helps on outdoor cooking which you will frequently find advertised in magazines.

Here are some old stand-bys for camping: *Camping and Woodcraft* by Horace Kephart (Macmillan). *Jack-Knife Cookery* by James Wilder (E. P. Dutton). *Woodcraft* and *The Junior Book of Camping and Woodcraft* by Bernard Mason (A. S. Barnes). *Games and Recreational Methods for Clubs, Camps, and Scouts* by Charles F. Smith (Dodd, Mead).

CHAPTER 15

Fireside Reading and
Campfire Activities

W HEN you sit by the fire alone, you may
want the companionship of a good book;
when you sit around a campfire, you look for the
companionship of other campers. Books and people are the right companions for armchair camping or for real camping. Sometimes you want
one, sometimes the other; sometimes you combine
them both in the plans you have for a campfire,
or for the unplanned, spontaneous things that
happen around a campfire.

We have suggested that there is much of
pioneer lore to help you know and enjoy outdoor
living; there are hundreds of other books that
you will enjoy, too; for any good yarn, any good
song, any poem of the out-of-doors will add to

the fellowship of a campfire. You'll soon find favorite anthologies or collections or individual
books that seem to make YOUR camping equipment complete. Here are a few suggestions of
books that campers like:

Stories of men and women who have camped
or traveled in canoes, in boats, on horseback, on
foot to unexplored country or little known
lands. *Canoe Country* by Florence Page Jaques is
an engaging story of outdoor life; *White Tower*
by James Ullman; *Cache Lake Country* by John
Rowlands; *High Jungle* by William Beebe are
other worthwhile books.

Nature stories—tales of the creatures that live
in the woods, the fields, the streams, or stories of
the people who have found adventure in fossil
beds, on mountain sides, in rivers or lakes, as they
discovered the wonders of the natural world.

Stories that are the folk lore of our country—
the tall tales of Paul Bunyan or the record of the
wandering Johnny Appleseed.

Stories that tell of the settling of the various
sections of our country—the American Mountain series, the Rivers of America series, and
others.

Stories of the people who have lived and
worked in the out-of-doors—Indians and sailors
and cowboys and lumbermen. You can get 35-
cent editions of *The Tattooed Man* by Howard
Pease; *Starbuck Valley Winter* by Roderick L.

Haig-Brown; *Forest Patrol* and *Big Red* by Jim Kjelgaard; (all COMET BOOKS) and *Ski Patrol* by Montgomery Atwater (a POCKET BOOK, JR.).

Nature poems and poems of the open are favorites with campers. There are anthologies that slip easily into pocket or knapsack; many campers like to make their own collections of poems that seem to describe a favorite spot or some happening on the trail. *The Nature Lover's Knapsack* compiled by E. O. Grover (Thomas Y. Crowell) is an especially good camper's collection.

Songs, too, are expressions of our feelings. There are songs for hiking, songs for quiet moments, songs that tell of the out-of-doors and of the people who have lived there. There are the songs we make up to tell our own adventures. There are songs that can be acted out, story songs, ceremonial songs, work songs. There are songs that describe outdoor things and outdoor feelings. Any good song is a good camping song, but some that have hiking rhythm or that fit into outdoor living seem to serve the campcrafter best.

ROUND THE CAMPFIRE

It's dusk—night is beginning to creep in—the fire lighter steps forward to touch off the blaze that will make the flames leap high. You all lean forward a little, in great anticipation of the nicest part of the camp day—CAMPFIRE TIME. If there are just a few of you, you may build up the dying cooking fire, stretch out around it, to swap yarns, sing a bit, or just sit and watch the flames. Campfires are the frosting of camping; you'll always remember the evenings in camp.

What happens at campfires? Well, almost anything, and there is no specified kind of program. Some are very informal, with nothing at all planned; some are ceremonials, with much preparation. In between are nights of fun which may include:

Singing—in small and large groups, or by one person. Rollicking songs, ballads, rounds, part songs, and quiet ones.

Music—especially with the instruments that help group singing or that are easily transported.

Dramatics—plays, ceremonies, informal and impromptu stunts, dramatized stories, poems and songs, puppets, pantomimes, etc.

Stories and yarns—told by a story teller, improvised by members of the group, read by some one; chronicles of the day's adventures, etc.

Games—guessing games, quiet games, trailing games, games that match wits, stunts that match strength, pencil and paper games.

Talks and pictures—by campers, foresters and naturalists who share their knowledge and their enthusiasm. Sometimes pictures add to their talks.

Discussions—planned or unplanned—on any subject.

Sometime when you are on a hosteling trip, you'll find other hostelers to share the peace of a campfire; sometime at a mountain shelter you'll meet some one whose harmonica just makes you sing; sometime at a forest campsite there will be some one who has had real adventure out of doors; sometime at a big campfire at a summer camp you'll discover the great joy of letting your own voice join in the singing of a crowd. Wherever it is, whatever you do, you will know the trail of camping has no equal in companionship, adventure and sheer fun. It will mean the finishing off of the hiking, the cooking out, the learning to use a knife or axe, the planning, the work and fun that have gone into your own campcrafter's trail—and you'll know that you will always be following a trail wherever you are, whatever you do.

For the Sunday cyclist... for the cross-country tourist... whether you ride for better health, for sport, or for the sheer fun of it,

GET

THE COMPLETE BOOK OF BICYCLING

The First Comprehensive Guide
To All Aspects of Bicycles and Bicycling

JUST A FEW OF THE HUNDREDS OF EXCITING TIPS YOU'LL FIND:

- A simple way to increase your cycling efficiency by 30 to 40%—breeze over hilltops while others are struggling behind.
- 13 special safety tips for youngsters.
- How to read a bicycle's specifications to know if you're getting a superior one or a dud.
- How to know whether to buy a 3-speed to start with, or a 10-speed.
- How to select the right kind of equipment for touring or camping.
- How to minimize danger when cycling in the city.

▼ AT YOUR BOOKSTORE OR MAIL THIS COUPON NOW FOR FREE 30-DAY TRIAL ▼

C4/1